Andrew Shitov

Using Raku

*100 Programming Challenges
Solved with
the Brand-New Raku
Programming Language*

2nd edition

DeepText — 2019

Using Raku
100 Programming Challenges Solved with
the Brand-New Raku Programming Language
© Andrew Shitov, author, 2019

This book is a collection of different programming challenges and solutions in Raku. It can be used as an exercise book, when you are learning Raku, or as a reference book when you are teaching it.

It is assumed that the reader knows the basics of Raku and wants to have some practice.

The 2nd edition published on 14th October 2019
The 1st edition published under the title "Using Perl 6" on 1st November 2017

Published by DeepText, Amsterdam
www.deeptext.media

ISBN 978-90-821568-8-1

Contents

Part 1

Chapter 1. Strings

1.1. Using strings

1.2. Modifying string data

Chapter 2. Numbers

Chapter 3. Aggregate Data Types

3.1. Manipulating lists and arrays

3.2. Information retrieval

3.3. Working with subroutines

Part 2

Chapter 5. Date and Time

Chapter 6. Parallel Computing

Chapter 7. Miscellaneous

Foreword

In this book, you will find 100 solutions of different common programming challenges that are written in Raku. Once you already know some of the basics of the language, it is a good idea to spend some time trying to do some exercises and the most popular tasks, which will vary from displaying the *Hello, World!* greeting, to creating a parser for the command-line calculator.

The seven chapters are divided into two parts, which cover the essential parts of the language; firstly, the strings, numbers, and aggregate data structures, and secondly, of Raku in particular, namely, the new regexes, grammars, and parallel computing.

Each of the 100 tasks presented in the book demonstrates the main idea of how to approach a problem; big chunks of code are avoided, as much as possible.

However, you are invited not to limit yourself to the proposed solution, though. First, try other approaches for the initial task, and then, extend the task with additional conditions and solve it. Do as many exercises in Raku as possible, because it will make you more fluent in this great language.

* * *

When reading this book, you should keep in mind that Raku is the language formerly known as Perl 6. When this book was published, the renaming process was in the very early phase, thus you will still see a lot of references to the Perl-related websites. It may take a few years for Raku name to replace Perl 6 completely.

Prerequisites

You need a Raku compiler. Visit rakudo.org and download the latest version of the Rakudo Star compiler. The code of the book works well with Rakudo Star version 2019.03, but you could use earlier versions down to 2017.09.

NB! To run Raku programs from the command line, you need to run the `raku` command (which, obviously, runs the compiler). In the meantime, before the rename is complete, you can either run the `perl6` command, or create an alias in your `.profile` file:

```
alias raku=perl6
```

You need a text editor, too. By default, Raku assumes that the source code is saved using UTF-8 encoding and, as some language constructs may use Unicode characters, it is better if your editor supports it.

If you are not yet familiar with Raku, read at least one of the following introductory books first:

Andrew Shitov, **Perl 6 at a Glance**
DeepText — 2017, ISBN 978-90-821568-3-6

Andrew Shitov, **Perl 6 Deep Dive**
Packt Publishing — 2017, ISBN 978-1-78728-204-9

If you need to improve your knowledge about programming in general, read another book, too:

Laurent Rosenfeld, Allen B. Downey, **Think Perl 6**
O'Reilly Media — 2017, ISBN 978-1-4919-8055-2

The source codes of all the examples in the book are located in the GitHub repository: github.com/ash/p6challenges.

How to debug programs

For quick tests, use the compiler in the mode of the REPL (*read—eval—print loop*) shell. Just run the raku command[1]:

```
$ raku
To exit type 'exit' or '^D'
>
```

With bigger programs, one of the following techniques helps to visualise data:

1. The `say` routine is used as a stand-alone function or as an object method. It works well with both scalar and aggregate data, such as arrays, hashes, or objects:

```
say $x;
%data.say;
```

3. The `WHAT` and the `^name` methods, which give you the information about the object type or class name:

```
my Int $x;
say $x.WHAT;   # (Int)
say $x.^name; # Int
```

4. The `dd` routine. This is a Rakudo-specific feature that dumps an object:

```
my @a = 1..5;
dd @a; # Array @a = [1, 2, 3, 4, 5]
```

---

[1] Before the rename is complete, use the `perl6` command or make an alias.

Part 1

Chapter 1

Strings

1.1

Using strings

1. Hello, World!

Print 'Hello, World!'

There are two built-in functions to print to the console: `print` and `say`. Both print their arguments, but the `say` routine additionally ends the output with a newline character.

So, the quickest solution is to use `say` and pass a string with no newlines:

```
say 'Hello, World!'
```

Another solution is to use `print` and include the \n character in the string itself:

```
print "Hello, World!\n"
```

The output of either program is the same:

```
Hello, World!
```

Notice the difference between single and double quotes: single quotes do not interpolate special characters like \n while the double quotes do. There's no mistake in using double quotes for strings without special characters, while it is better to use the appropriate quoting style when you do not expect variables in the string and when there is no need to interpolate variables.

Another thing to take a look at in the examples above is that a semicolon is not required for one-line programs.

2. Greet a person

Ask a user for their name and greet them by printing 'Hello, <Name>!'

Raku offers a simple `prompt` function that performs both actions: prints a prompt and reads the input. So, the program using it may look like this:

```
say 'Hello, ' ~ prompt('Enter your name: ') ~ '!';
```

The ~ operator stands for string concatenation. Don't be confused by the sequence of text strings in this code. To build the string, Raku needs to have all its parts. Two of them (`'Hello'`, and `'!'`) are presented by literal strings, while the middle part needs user input. Therefore, the flow of the whole program remains logical:

```
Enter your name: Andy
Hello, Andy!
```

If you prefer a more traditional program flow, split it into separate parts and interpolate a variable in a string:

```
my $name = prompt('Enter your name: ');
say "Hello, $name!";
```

Alternatively, the `get` function may be used. It returns the input line without the newline character. Printing a prompt message is your responsibility now:

```
print 'Enter your name: ';
my $name = get();
say "Hello, $name!";
```

The `get` function may be called as a method on the `$*IN` variable, which is by default connected to the standard input:

```
my $name = $*IN.get();
```

3. String length

Print the length of a string.

The Raku language handles all strings as UTF-8 by default. This is why there is more than one parameter describing the length of the string. In fact, the `length` routine does not exist, and an attempt to use it issues an error message with some hints to which other methods you can use.

To get the length of the string in the sense of number of characters, use the `chars` method:

```
say 'hello'.chars;  # 5
say 'café'.chars;   # 4
say 'привет'.chars; # 6
```

The results reflect the intuitive expectation and do not depend on actual representation of the characters. The first string fits in the ASCII table, the second may still be encoded in an 8-bit encoding Latin-1, and the third needs two bytes per character in the UTF-8 encoding.

Another method, `codes`, returns the number of codepoints in the Unicode space. For the above examples, both `chars` and `codes` return the same numbers, as all the characters can be represented by a single codepoint.

```
say 'hello'.codes;  # 5
say 'café'.codes;   # 4
say 'привет'.codes; # 6
```

Although, when using combining characters, you may create a character that does not exist as a separate character in the Unicode table. In this case, the results of `chars` and `codes` may differ.

Consider an example with a character built out of two elements: Latin letter x and a combining character COMBINING OGONEK. Together, they form a non-existing letter, which is one character, but two codepoints:

```
say 'x̨'.chars; # 1
say 'x̨'.codes; # 2
```

Let us dig a bit into how the above character is represented in the UTF-8 encoding. It consists of two parts: LATIN SMALL LETTER X and the combining character COMBINING OGONEK. The letter itself is a one-byte code 0x78, and the combining character has the Unicode entry point 0x328 and needs two bytes in UTF-8: 0xCC 0xA8.

Let us rewrite the example by explicitly specifying the codepoint of the combining character:

```
say "x\x[0328]".chars; # 1
say "x\x[0328]".codes; # 2
```

The above example was about the character that does not exist in Unicode as a single codepoint. Now, let us use another letter, say e, which forms an existing character with the same combining character: ę.

```
say 'ę'.chars; # 1
say 'ę'.codes; # 1
```

In this case, both chars and codes methods return 1. Even if the string is built using an explicit combining character, the codes method coerces it back to the proper codepoint and does not count it as a separate code:

```
say "e\x[0328]".chars; # 1
say "e\x[0328]".codes; # 1
```

Thus, in many cases, to get the length of a string, it is enough to use the chars method called on that string.

4. Unique digits

Print unique digits from a given integer number.

The task is easily solved if an integer is immediately converted to a string.

```
my $number = prompt('Enter number> ');
say $number.comb.unique.sort.join(', ');
```

The `comb` method, called with no arguments, splits the string into separate characters. The method is defined in the `Str` class; thus, the `$number` is converted to the string first. The same may be explicitly written as:

```
$number.Str.comb
```

Notice that in the case of using `$number.split('')`, empty elements are added to the beginning and the end of the array.

At this moment, an initial number resides in an array, each element of which is a digit from the `$number`.

Taking unique elements of an array does not require any manual programming, as the `Array` class contains a special method for that:

```
$number.comb.unique
```

Finally, to make the result look better, the array of unique digits is sorted and printed as a comma-separated list:

```
$number.comb.unique.sort.join(', ')
```

Instead of calling `say` as a stand-alone function, it may be called as a method on the resulting string:

```
$number.comb.unique.sort.join(', ').say;
```

1.2

Modifying string data

5. Reverse a string

Print a string in the reversed order from right to left.

Strings, or the objects of the `Str` class, have the `flip` method, which does the work:

```
my $string = 'Hello, World!';
say $string.flip;
```

This code prints the desired result:

```
!dlroW ,olleH
```

The `flip` routine may be called both as a method on a string and as a stand-alone function:

```
say flip 'Abcdef'; # fedcbA
say 'Word'.flip;   # droW
```

Don't forget that `say` can also be called as a method:

```
'Magic'.flip.say; # cigaM
```

There is also the `reverse` routine, but it cannot be applied directly to strings. It accepts lists, so a string first has to be converted to the list of characters, then reversed, and later joined again to a string.

Here is the code that works according to this description.

```
my $string = 'Hello, World!';
my $reversed = $string.split('').reverse().join('');
say $reversed; # !dlroW ,olleH
```

6. Removing blanks from a string

Remove leading, trailing and double spaces from a given string.

This task often occurs when you need to clean the user input, such as from web forms, where leading or trailing spaces in, for example, names, are most likely user mistakes and should be removed.

Removing double and multiple spaces between words can be solved by using substitution:

```
my $string = 'Hello,      World!';
$string ~~ s:g/\s+/ /;
```

Don't forget to make the substitution global with the `:g` adverb to find all the occurrences of repeated spaces.

Leading and trailing spaces can be removed with the `trim` routine:

```
my $string = ' Hello, World! ';
say trim($string);
```

The `trim` routine exists as a self-standing function, as shown in the previous example, as well as a method of the `Str` class, so it can be called on a variable or on a string:

```
say $string.trim;
say ' Hello, World! '.trim;
```

There are also two routines, `trim-leading` and `trim-trailing`, which remove either only leading or only trailing spaces.

```
say '¡' ~ ' Hi  '.trim-leading;  # ¡Hi␣ ␣
say '  Hi  '.trim-trailing ~ '!'; # ␣ ␣Hi!
```

7. Camel case

Create a camel-case identifier from a given phrase.

It is a good practice to follow some pattern when choosing names for variables, functions, and classes in any programming language. In Raku, identifiers are case-sensitive, and, unlike many other languages, hyphens are allowed. So, variables names like `$max-span` or function names like `celsius-to-fahrenheit` are accepted.

In this task, we will form the `CamelCase` variable names from a given phrase. Names created in this style are built of several words; each of which starts with a capital letter.

Here's the program that does the required conversions:

```
my $text = prompt('Enter short text > ');
my $CamelName = $text.comb(/\w+/).map({.tclc}).join('');
say $CamelName;
```

All the actions are done in a sequence of method calls. The words are selected from the input `$text` using the `comb` method with a regex `/\w+/`. Then, each found word is `mapped` using the `tclc` method, which is equivalent to the chained call `.lc.tc`:

A 'bare' dot means that the method is called on the default variable `$_`, which is repeatedly set to the current element. In Raku, there is no `ucfirst` method to make the first letter of the text uppercase. Instead, we are using the `tclc` method; *tc* stands for *Title Case*, *lc* for *Lower Case*, and all the letters are converted to lowercase except the first one.

Finally, the elements of the array are joined together with the help of the `join` method. The input string 'Hello, World!' becomes `HelloWord` after all the transformations are done.

8. Incrementing filenames

Generate a list of filenames like file1.txt, file2.txt, etc.

Raku allows incrementing those kinds of filenames directly:

```
my $filename = 'file0.txt';
for 1..5 {
    $filename++;
    say $filename;
}
```

This program prints the list of consequent filenames:

```
file1.txt
file2.txt
file3.txt
file4.txt
file5.txt
```

Notice that after reaching 9, the *e* letter from *file* is incremented. Thus, `file9.txt` is followed by `filf0.txt`. To prevent that, add enough zeros in the template:

```
my $filename = 'file000.txt';
for 1..500 {
    $filename++;
    say $filename;
}
```

Now, the sequence starts with `file001.txt` and continues to `file500.txt`.

Multiple file extensions in the template, say `file000.tar.gz`, are also handled properly, so the numeric part is incremented.

9. Random passwords

Generate a random string that can be used as a password.

One of the possible solutions looks like this:

```
say ('0' .. 'z').pick(15).join('');
```

The `pick` method with no arguments takes a random element from the range of the ASCII characters between `0` and `z`. In the above example, calling `pick(15)` selects 15 different characters, which are then joined together using the `join` method.

It is important to know the two key features of the `pick` method. First, when called with an integer argument bigger than 1, the result contains only unique elements. Thus, all the characters in the password are different.

The second feature is a consequence of the first one. If the provided list of elements is not long enough, and its length is less than the argument of `pick`, the result is as long as the original data list.

To see which elements are used for generating a password, run the code with a number bigger than the whole ASCII sequence:

```
say ('0' .. 'z').pick(1000).sort.join('');
```

With this request, you will see all the characters that participate in forming a random password:

```
0123456789:;<=>?@ABCDEFGHIJKLMNOPQRSTUVWXYZ[\]^_`
abcdefghijklmnopqrstuvwxyz
```

An example of a generated password: `05<EV]^bdfhnpyz`.

To limit the character range, list the characters you want to see in a password:

```
my @chars = '0' ... '9', 'A' ... 'Z', 'a' ... 'z';
say @chars.pick(15).join('');
```

Now the password only contains alphanumeric symbols: 2zOIySp5PHb08Ql.

The ... operator creates a sequence. Be warned not to use the .. operator, which creates a range, in which case the @chars array is an array of ranges rather than a flat array of single characters.

The solution is quite elegant and does not require explicit use of the rand function. Neither loops are needed.

Now, let us solve the task in such a way that characters may be repeated in the result. It is still possible to use the pick method but it should be called independently a few times.

```
my $password = '';
$password ~= ('0' .. 'z').pick() for 1..15;
say $password;
```

Now, the password can include the same character more than once, for example: jn@09Icoys@tD;o.

To get the string of unique characters, use the pick method instead of roll. When using roll, you have to make sure the source list of characters is bigger than the length of your password.

```
my $password = '';
$password ~= ('0' .. 'z').roll() for 1..15;
say $password;
```

Run the code a few times to confirm that you generate good passwords that are all different and do not contain the same characters more than once.

10. DNA-to-RNA transcription

Convert the given DNA sequence to a compliment RNA.

We'll not dig deep into the biology aspect of the problem. For us, it is important that the DNA is a string containing the four letters A, C, G, and T, and the RNA is a string of A, C, G, and U. The transformation from DNA to RNA happens according to the following table:

DNA	A	C	G	T
RNA	U	G	C	A

In the `Str` class, the `trans` method is defined; it takes pairs 'old character—new character'. So, to translate from DNA to RNA, let's write the above table as a hash and use it with the `trans` method:

```
my %transcription =
    A => 'U', C => 'G', G => 'C', T => 'A';

my $dna = 'ACCATCAGTC';
my $rna = $dna.trans(%transcription);
say $rna; # UGGUAGUCAG
```

The `trans` method accepts a few attributes that alternate its behaviour. For example, the `:squash` attribute removes the duplicated characters. This probably does not make sense in biology, but works for us an exercise:

```
say $dna.trans(%transcription, :squash); # UGUAGUCAG
```

It is also possible to replace the sequences of more than one character. For example:

```
say $dna.trans('ACCA' => 'UGGU', 'TCA' => 'AGU',
               'GTC' => 'CAG');
```

11. Caesar cipher

Encode a message using the Caesar cipher technique.

The Caesar code is a simple method of transcoding the letters of the message so that each letter is replaced with the letter that occurs in the alphabet N positions earlier or later.

For example, if N is 4, then the letter *e* becomes *a*, *f* is transformed to *b*, etc. The alphabet is looped so that *z* becomes *v*, and letters *a* to *d* become *w* to *z*.

The `Str` data type is equipped with the `trans` method, which we have seen in Task 10, *DNA-to-RNA transcription*. It is also quite easy to use ranges in the replacement recipe:

```
my $message = 'hello, world!';

my $secret = $message.trans(
                ['a' .. 'z'] =>
                ['w' .. 'z', 'a' .. 'v']
            );
say $secret; # dahhk, sknhz!
```

You can read the original message by translating it back with the same method but with swapped arrays:

```
say $secret.trans(
    ['w' .. 'z', 'a' .. 'v'] =>
    ['a' .. 'z']
);
```

Try modifying the solution so that it also works with the strings containing capital letters.

1.3

Text analysis

12. Plural endings

Put a noun in the correct form—singular or plural—depending on the number next to it.

In program outputs, it is often required to print some number followed by a noun, for example:

```
10 files copied
```

If there is only one file, then the phrase should be '`1 file copied`' instead. Let's see how the language can help.

Of course, it is quite easy to print a noun separately using string concatenation to make the whole phrase:

```
for 1, 2, 3 -> $n {                    # Program output:
    my $word = 'file';                 # 1 file found
    $word ~= 's' if $n > 1;            # 2 files found
    say "$n $word found";              # 3 files found
}
```

It is also a good practice to interpolate the word choice into the string itself to avoid additional lines of code and to get rid of temporary variables.

The following program generates the same output:

```
for 1, 2, 3 -> $n {
    say "$n file{'s' if $n > 1} found";
}
```

A code block in curly braces inside the string contains a regular Raku code. It returns `'s'` if the number `$n` is greater than one. Notice that there is no need to use a ternary operator here; a postfix `if` looks very self-explaining.

13. The most frequent word

Find the most frequent word in the given text.

To find the most frequent word, you need first to find all the words in the text.

This can be done via the global regex `m:g/(\w+)/` or by using the `comb` method. The method returns a list of all the matched substrings. In the following example of solving the task, the regex matching is placed inside the `for` loop, which immediately updates the `%count` hash, which keeps the number of occurrences of each found word. To allow counting words case-insensitively, the `$text` value is first lower-cased with the help of the `lc` string method.

```
my $text = prompt('Text> ');
my %count;
%count{$_}++ for $text.lc.comb(/\w+/);
say (sort {%count{$^b} <=> %count{$^a}}, %count.keys)[0];
```

The `sort` function sorts the hash using the word frequency as the sorting parameter. Then, the first element, `[0]`, is taken and printed.

Test the program on different texts to see how it works. What you may notice is that the program always prints only one word, even if there are other words with the same number of occurrences. To solve the problem, extract the number of repetitions and filter the `%count` hash to find all the words that match this condition.

```
my $max = %count{(sort {%count{$^b} <=> %count{$^a}},
                count.keys)[0]};
.say for %count.keys.grep({%count{$_} == $max});
```

This program prints all the words having the maximum values in `%count`.

14. The longest common substring

Find the longest common substring in the given two strings.

Let us limit ourselves with finding only the first longest substring. If there
are more common substrings of the same length, then the rest are ignored.
There are two loops (see also Task 17, *The longest palindrome*) over the first
string ($a), and they use the index method to search for the substring in the
second string ($b).

```
my $a = 'the quick brown fox jumps over the lazy dog';
my $b = 'what does the fox say?';

my $common = '';
for 0 .. $a.chars -> $start {
    for $start ..^ $a.chars -> $end {
        my $s = $a.substr($start, $a.chars - $end);
        if $s.chars > $common.chars && $b.index($s).defined {
            $common = $s;
        }
    }
}

say $common
    ?? "The longest common substring is '$common'."
    !! 'There are no common substrings.';
```

The index method returns the position of the substring $s if it is found in
the string $b. It is a little bit tricky to check if the substring is found because
when it is found at the beginning of the string, then the returned value is 0
(as 0 is the position of the substring). If the substring is not found, then Nil
is returned. Nil is not a numeric value; thus, it cannot be compared using
the == or != operators. Use the defined method to check if index returns a
value, not Nil: $b.index($s).defined.

15. Anagram test

Tell if the two words are anagrams of each other.

Anagrams are words or phrases that are built out of the same letters. We start with checking words only.

```
my $a = prompt('First word > ');
my $b = prompt('Second word > ');

say normalize($a) eq normalize($b)
    ?? 'Anagrams.' !! 'Not anagrams.';

sub normalize($word) {
    return $word.comb.sort.join('');
}
```

The words, stored in the `$a` and `$b` variables, are passed through the `normalize` function, which converts a word into a string, where all the letters are alphabetically sorted. For example, the 'hello' string becomes 'ehllo'. If both words can be normalised to the same form, they are anagrams.

To make the program accept phrases, let's modify the `normalize` function so that it removes the spaces from the phrase and makes all the letters lowercase:

```
sub normalize($word) {
    return $word.lc.comb.sort.join('').trans(' ' => '');
}
```

There are two additions to the above chain of method calls: `lc` converts the string to the lowercase version, and the `trans` method replaces all the spaces with an empty string. After these changes, the 'Hello World' phrase becomes 'dehllloorw'.

16. Palindrome test

Check if the entered string is palindromic.

A palindrome is a string that can be read from both ends: left to right or right
to left. First, start with the simple case when the string contains only letters.
(Thus, spaces and punctuation do not affect anything.)

In Task 5, *Reverse a string*, the `flip` method is used to reverse a string. To
check whether it is a palindrome, compare the string with its flipped version.

```
my $string = prompt('Enter a string: ');
my $is_palindrome = $string eq $string.flip;

say 'The string is ' ~
    (!$is_palindrome ?? 'not ' !! '') ~
    'palindromic.';
```

This code works well with single words like *ABBA* or *madam* or *kayak*.

Let us take the next step and teach the program to work with sentences that
contain spaces and punctuation characters. For removing all the non-letter
characters, regexes are a good choice:

```
$string ~~ s:g/\W+//;
```

The `\W+` regex matches with all non-word characters. All occurrences of
them are removed from the string (replaced with nothing). The `:g` adverb
tells the regex to repeatedly scan the whole string.

Additionally, the string should be lowercased:

```
$string .= lc;
```

The `lc` method is called on `$string`, and the result is assigned back to the same variable. This construction is equivalent to the following:

```
$string = $string.lc;
```

Add these two lines to the program:

```
my $string = prompt('Enter a string: ');

$string ~~ s:g/\W+//;
$string .= lc;

my $is_palindrome = $string eq $string.flip;

say 'The string is ' ~
    (!$is_palindrome ?? 'not ' !! '') ~
    'palindromic.';
```

Check the modified program against a few random sentences and a few palindromes:

Never odd or even.

Was it a rat I saw?

Mr. Owl ate my metal worm.

That's all. As an additional stroke, it is a good thing to simplify the concatenated string a bit and use interpolation:

```
my $string = prompt('Enter a string: ');
$string ~~ s:g/\W+//;
$string .= lc;

my $is_palindrome = $string eq $string.flip;
my $not = $is_palindrome ?? '' !! ' not';
say "The string is$not palindromic.";
```

17. The longest palindrome

Find the longest palindromic substring in the given string.

The main idea behind the solution is to scan the string with a window of varying width. In other words, starting from a given character, test all the substrings of any length possible at that position.

For the string `$string`, this is how the loops can be organized:

```
for 0 .. $length -> $start {
    for $start .. $length - 1 -> $end {
        . . .
    }
}
```

Now, extract the substring using the `substr` method, which is defined for the objects of the `Str` type, and do the check similar to the solution of Task 16, *Palindrome test*. Here, we have to be careful to check the palindrome without taking into account the non-letter characters but saving the result as part of the original string. For this, a copy of the substring is made.

```
my $substring = $string.substr($start, $length - $end);
my $test = $substring;
$test ~~ s:g/\W+//;
$test .= lc;
if $test eq $test.flip && $substring.chars > $found.chars {
    $found = $substring;
}
```

The temporary result is saved in the `$found` variable. The algorithm keeps track of the first longest palindromic substring. If there are more than one such substrings of the same length, they are ignored.

Here is the complete code of the program.

```
my $string = prompt('Enter string> ');
my $length = $string.chars;
my $found = '';

for 0 .. $length -> $start {
    for $start .. $length - 1 -> $end {
        my $substring =
            $string.substr($start, $length - $end);
        my $test = $substring;
        $test ~~ s:g/\W+//;
        $test .= lc;
        if $test eq $test.flip &&
            $substring.chars > $found.chars {
            $found = $substring;
        }
    }
}

if $found {
    say "The longest substring is '$found'.";
}
else {
    say "No palindromic substrings found.";
}
```

Run the program and see how it works.

```
Enter string> Hello, World!
The longest substring is 'o, Wo'.
```

As homework, modify the code so that it can track more than one palindromic substrings of the same length. It may, for example, keep the candi-
dates in an array and re-initialize it if a longer palindrome is found.

18. Finding duplicate texts

Find duplicate fragments in the same text.

This task was dictated by the practical need when I realised that I used the same phrases in different parts of the text of this book. Some of them, like *Hello, World!*, are unavoidable, but it would be a great help to find the rest.

Here is the full solution, which scans the text from standard input and finds the sequences of *N* words which appear more than once in the text.

```
my $text = $*IN.slurp;
$text .= lc;
$text ~~ s:g/\W+/ /;
my $length = $text.chars;


my %phrases;
my $start = 0;
while $text ~~ m:c($start)/(<< [\w+] ** 5 %% \s >>) .+ $0/ {
    $start = $0.from + 1;
    %phrases{$0}++;

    print (100 * $start / $length).fmt('%i%% ');
    say $0;
}


say "\nDuplicated strings:";

for %phrases.keys.sort({%phrases{$^b} <=> %phrases{$^a}}) {
    say "$_ = " ~ %phrases{$_} + 1;
}
```

The program is relatively complicated, so let us examine it bit by bit.

First, the program reads the input using the `$*IN.slurp` call that returns the whole input text. It reads all the lines and creates a single string variable out of it. The `.=lc` method, called on the `$text` variable, makes the string lowercase and also assigns it back to the variable.

With a substitution `s/\W+/ /`, all non-alphanumeric sequences are replaced with a space. Thus, we eliminate all the punctuation, for example.

The last step of preparatory work is to save the length of the text in a variable so that we use it later in the program directly, instead of calling the `chars` method (see Task 3, *String length*).

Now, the main loop starts. Its goal is to take all the five-word sequences that occur at least twice in the text and place them in the `%phrases` hash. Each time another copy of the phrase is found, the value in the `%phrases` hash is incremented. At the end of the loop, the hash contains the number of occurrences for each such five-word sequence.

Look at the regex that finds the repetitions:

```
m:c($start)/(<< [\w+] ** 5 %% \s >>) .+ $0/
```

The main part of it, `<< [\w+] ** 5 %% \s >>`, finds five words separated by a space. The `<<` and `>>` anchors stick to word boundaries, `[\w+ ** 5]` is a sequence of five words, and the separator is mentioned in the `%%` clause: `%% \s`. The regex then needs a copy of the just matched phrase, and this is the job of the `$0` variable inside the regex.

Finally, the `:c` adverb with a parameter—the `$start` value—makes the regex match against the string starting the `$start` position. This counter is incremented in the loop body based on the location of the first found phrase: `$start = $0.from + 1`.

The rest of the program prints the result as a table. It sorts the found phrases and displays the most frequent first.

Chapter 2

Numbers

2.1

Using numbers

19. π

Print the value of π.

The value of π is accessible with no additional modules:

```
say π;
```

This instruction, not a surprise, prints the desired value:

```
3.14159265358979
```

As you may have noticed, a non-ASCII character was used in the code. Raku assumes that the source code is encoded as UTF-8 by default. Instead, a non-Unicode version can be used, too:

```
say pi;
```

There are a couple more built-in constants: `tau` and `e`; both of them have Unicode variants: τ and e (character code `0x1D452`):

```
say τ;
say e;
```

The value of `tau` is equal to 2π, and the above program prints the following result:

```
6.28318530717959
2.71828182845905
```

It is also worth knowing that there's a special constant for presenting infinity: `Inf` or ∞. This number is bigger than any other (reasonably big) number; either an integer or a floating-point value.

```
say 1E120 < ∞; # Prints True
```

20. Factorial!

Print the factorial of a given number.

By definition, the factorial of a positive integer number *N* is a product of all the integers numbering from 1 to *N*, including *N*. This can be easily expressed with the use of a reduction operator:

```
my $n = 5;
my $f = [*] 1 .. $n;
say $f;
```

The record `[*] 1 .. $n` is equivalent to the following expression:

```
1 * 2 * 3 * 4 * ... * ($n - 1) * $n
```

A compact form `[*]` means that the operation character * is placed between the numbers in the given list.

The result in the case of `$n` equals 5 is:

```
120
```

Another approach to calculating factorials is using recursion according to the formula:

$$n! = n \cdot (n - 1)!$$

On each iteration step, the function calls itself with decremented argument and should stop as soon as the value becomes less than two. In Raku, the knowledge of the fact that 1! is 1 can be encoded as a special case using multi-functions.

Multi-functions are subroutines prefixed with the `multi` keyword. They all share the name but may be distinguished by the type, number or values of their arguments.

For the factorial, define two multi-functions, one to calculate the factorial of the smallest numbers 0 and 1 (ignore the negative numbers for now):

```
multi sub factorial(Int $x where {$x < 2}) {
    return 1;
}
```

The second variant is for all the other numbers.

```
multi sub factorial(Int $x) {
    return $x * factorial($x - 1);
}
```

The `where` clause in the function signature splits the calls to the `factorial` functions. It is enough to have the `where` clause only in one of the two function variants, but you can explicitly add it for clarity: `where $x >= 2`.

Calling the factorial with the number 5 calls the second variant a few times first, switching to the first variant when `$x` reaches `1`. As that variant does not iteratively call itself, the whole recursion loop stops.

```
say factorial(5);
```

Take a look at the signature of the function:

```
(Int $x where {$x < 2})
```

Here, the variable `$x` is typed as `Int` (which is an integer in Raku) and restricted by the condition `{$x < 2}` in the `where` clause. Therefore, this signature does its work to decide if the corresponding subroutine accepts the number or not.

Raku offers another exciting thing, which gives quite impressive results in its application to the factorial task. It is possible to define your own postfix operators, so you can write 5! in the code and get the factorial of five.

Here is an example of defining the postfix ! operator:

```
sub postfix:<!>($n) {
    return [*] 1 .. $n;
}
```

Using it is straightforward:

```
say 5!;
```

This factorial operator is also applicable to variables, including the default variable:

```
my $x = 7;
say $x!;  # Prints 5040

say .! for 3..7;  # 6, 24, 120, 720, 5040
```

Recursive definition works with the user-defined operator, too. It is possible to use it even from the body of the operator definition itself:

```
sub postfix:<!>($n) {
    $n <= 1 ?? 1 !! $n * ($n - 1)!
}

say 5!;  # Prints 120
```

The stop condition of the recursion is implemented here via the Boolean check $n <= 1. In one-line functions like those shown above, it is not necessary to type the return keyword, as the last calculated value is used as the result.

21. Fibonacci numbers

Print the Nth Fibonacci number.

Fibonacci numbers are defined by the recurring formula:

$$f_n = f_{n-1} + f_{n-2}.$$

You can assign two values at a time (see Task 48, *Swap two values*). You can use that technique for calculating the next Fibonacci number from the previous two. To bootstrap the algorithm, the two first values are needed. In one of the definitions of the Fibonacci row, the first two values are both 1 (sometimes, you may see that the first number is 0).

```
my ($a, $b) = (1, 1);
($a, $b) = ($b, $a + $b) for 3 .. 10;
say $b;
```

Another way of generating the sequence is to use the *sequence operator*. With this operator, you create a lazy list, which calculates its values according to the formula given in the generator argument.

```
my @fib = 1, 1, * + * ... *;
say @fib[9];
```

The @fib array is a sequence. Its first two elements are both 1, but the rest are defined by the formula * + *. This code creates an anonymous block that is equivalent to the body of a function with two arguments: {$a + $b}. Thus, the element is a sum of its two neighbours. The right end of the sequence is specified as *, which means that it generates numbers infinitely, based on the demand.

The next line just takes the 10th element of the array and prints its value:

55

22. Print squares

Print the squares of the numbers from 1 to 10.

To print the squares for a range of numbers, a loop is required. If the body of the loop is simple, you can use the postfix notation:

```
say $_ ** 2 for 1..10;
```

The `$_` variable is a loop variable, which receives the new value on each iteration.

Raku offers the `**` operator for calculating powers, so it can be used instead of the straightforward multiplication `$_ * $_`.

In the case of you needing a named loop variable, choose another form of a loop:

```
for 1..10 -> $x {
    say $x * $x;
}
```

Notice that there are no parentheses around the range in the `for` loop.

We also can create a list of squares using the `map` function, as demonstrated in the following example:

```
.say for map {$_ ** 2}, 1..10;
```

Here, the range `1..10` is first converted to the list, each element of which is a square of the corresponding element of the initial list, and then it is printed one by one as before.

The dot before `say` means calling the `say` method on the default variable, so both `$_.say` and `.say` are equivalent.

23. Powers of two

Print the first ten powers of two.

The naïve loop for calculating powers of two can be created similar to the solution of the Task 22, *Print squares*:

```
say 2 ** $_ for 0..9;
```

It prints the values 1, 2, 4, etc. up to 512.

There's another way of generating sequences with the defined rule of calculating its elements:

```
my @power2 = 1, 2, {$_ * 2} ... *;
.say for @power2[^10];
```

The rule here is {$_ * 2}, so each next number is twice as big as the previous one. The @power2 array gets the values of the infinite lazy list, and only the first ten elements are used for printing. The ^10 construction at the place of array index creates a range 0..9, and the corresponding slice of @power2 is taken.

Raku also can deduce the rule if you provide the first few elements of the list:

```
my @power2 = 1, 2, 4 ... *;
.say for @power2[^10];
```

In the less obvious cases, you'd better prefer an explicit generator for lazy lists.

24. Odd and even numbers

Print the first ten odd numbers. Print the first ten even numbers.

Odd numbers are those that have a remainder after division by 2. This fact can be directly exploited in filtering the numbers and printing only those that match this definition.

```
.say if $_ % 2 for 1 .. 20;
```

To print even numbers, negate the condition by choosing another keyword: `unless`, instead of `if`:

```
.say unless $_ % 2 for 1 .. 20;
```

Numbers can be filtered using the `grep` built-in function:

```
.say for grep {$_ % 2}, 1..20;
```

For the odd numbers, negate the condition by using the divisibility operator, which returns `True` when its first operand is divisible by the second with no remainder:

```
.say for grep {$_ %% 2}, 1..20;
```

Another interesting approach is using a sequence. Show the first elements of it, and the rest are generated automatically:

```
my @odd = 1, 3 ... *;
say @odd[^10];
```

To print the even numbers, change the sample:

```
my @even = 2, 4 ... *;
say @even[^10];
```

25. Compare numbers approximately

Compare the two non-integer values approximately.

Comparing non-integer numbers, which are represented as floating-point numbers is often a task that requires approximate comparison.

There is the =~= operator, called the *approximately-equal operator*, which checks if its operands are close enough to each other.

```
say 1/1000 =~= 1/1001;          # False
say 1/1E20 =~= 1 / (1E20 + 1);  # True
```

The result of the approximate comparison is True if the difference is less than the value set in the $*TOLERANCE constant, which is equal to 1E-15.

Notice that in Raku, a number in a scientific notation is a floating-point number, while other representations, such as 0.5 or 1/2, or <1/2>, or even ½, are the values of the Rat type (*Rat* stands for *rational*).

Rational numbers are stored as two integer values, the numerator and the denominator. Computations with such numbers, therefore, do not loose accuracy. Compare the results of the following classical example, with a similar program in other languages:

```
say 0.1 + 0.2 - 0.3; # 0
```

Raku prints an exact zero, even if you try to print the result with many digits after the decimal point:

```
'%.20f'.printf(0.1 + 0.2 - 0.3); # 0.00000000000000000000
```

This is very nice of Raku, isn't it?

26. Multiplying big numbers

Create a program to multiply very big integer numbers.

The support for big numbers is built-in: the Int class allows arbitrary precision. You do not have to do any extra work. You just take the numbers and multiply them, as shown in the example (numbers should be written on one line, and without spaces, of course):

```
my $a =
    8327493849387483265832732094834978362483947968329746348
    3724632869485324609897469328493826439284973286563298782
    4639847823659328476832647392847836539843928645384329463
    28753924837825643824302487637563724384782374803284710339876;

my $b =
    2384938952039487410030293547034085109432785279287346539
    2342359923402340327532493254901109323484587883023847982
    3384973572956827684982039857845823094878574509385476502
    023495845208724875429387529305925742958437568398454386 7549;

say $a * $b;
```

Run the program and check the result :-)

```
$ raku multiply.rk
19860564454273461346088164616741048177096180676214308595632079
41437226572258175727633535561316010373307679877834702680894647
64504400339607310787754299375646554963128327698080593673173156
71123225436954086384610546927999627107170630456325629536616550
28129020817093482213746516429627686325589675507869799601220291
14902545655702554835467523365237055296210216509834632137632579
49051914269400329363303739250954927419262331885811166410164223
077073317083924
```

57

27. Prime numbers

Decide if the given number is a prime number.

Prime numbers are those that can be divided only by 1, and by themselves.

The language provides us with a built-in support, the `is-prime` routine, for checking if the number is prime. There are two ways of using it.

First, as a built-in function:

```
say 'Prime' if is-prime(17);
```

Second, as a method on an object of the `Int` type:

```
my $n = 15;
say $n.is-prime
    ?? "$n is prime"
    !! "$n is not prime"
    ;
```

Here, the ternary operator ?? ... !! is used. This code prints either of the strings, depending on the result of calling `$n.is-prime`:

```
17 is prime
```

```
15 is not prime
```

Notice that the `is-prime` routine contains a hyphen in its name, which is a valid character for identifier names in Raku.

28. List of prime numbers

Print the list of the first ten prime numbers.

In Task 27, *Prime numbers*, we've seen how to check if the given number is prime. To print the list of the first ten numbers, organize a lazy list. The code is quite compact:

```
my @numbers = grep {.is-prime}, 1..*;
say @numbers[^10];
```

The first line has to be read from right to left. The lazy list `1..*` is filtered with the grep function, and another lazy list resides in the `@numbers` variable.

Then, the first ten elements are taken and printed:

```
(2 3 5 7 11 13 17 19 23 29)
```

It is possible to use the colon to pass arguments to functions. The above-shown code can be rewritten differently:

```
my @numbers = (1..*).grep: *.is-prime;
say @numbers[^10];
```

Notice that the two usages of * mean different things here. The range of `1..*` is replaceable with an open-end range `^∞` or `^Inf`.

```
my @numbers = (^Inf).grep: *.is-prime;
say @numbers[^10];
```

Finally, make a selection of the first ten elements directly:

```
say ((^∞).grep: *.is-prime)[^10];
```

29. Prime factors

Find the prime factors of a given number.

Prime factors are the prime numbers that divide the given integer number exactly.

In Task 28, *List of prime numbers,* we've seen how to make a lazily evaluated list of prime numbers. This list is used in the program as a generator of the factor numbers for the tests.

```
my $n = 123456789;

my @list;
my @prime = grep {.is-prime}, 1..*;
my $pos = 0;

while $n > 1 {
    my $factor = @prime[$pos];
    $pos++;
    next unless $n %% $factor;

    $pos = 0;
    $n /= $factor;
    push @list, $factor;
}

say @list; # [3 3 3607 3803]
```

On each iteration, the number is tested with the $n %% $factor condition. If the factor has been found, it is added to the @list array, the current position in the @prime arrays is set back to 0 (because factors may repeat), and the number $n is divided by the $factor value before the next iteration. The loop finishes when the value of $n becomes equal to 1.

30. Reducing a fraction

Compose a fraction from the two given integers—numerator and denominator—and reduce it to lowest terms.

5/15 and 16/280 are examples of fractions that can be reduced. The final results of this task are 1/3 and 2/35. Generally, the algorithm of reducing a fraction requires searching for the greatest common divisor, and then dividing both numerator and denominator by that number.

There is a built-in operator `gcd` that returns the greatest common divisor, so you can use it to solve the task (notice that `gcd` is used as an operator, not a function):

```
my $a = 16;
my $b = 280;

my $gcd = $a gcd $b;
say $a/$gcd; # 2
say $b/$gcd; # 35
```

That is a classical solution, but Raku offers something much more magical—the Rational data type `Rat`.

```
my Rat $r = $a/$b;
say $r.numerator;   # 2
say $r.denominator; # 35
```

The `Rat` value keeps its parts as two integers, which are accessible via the numerator and denominator methods. The `dd` routine gives you the instant insight:

```
dd $r;  # Rat $r = <2/35>
```

31. Divide by zero

Do something with the division by zero.

Division by zero in itself is not an immediate error in Raku.

The following code does not generate an exception and prints the message after the problematic division.

```
my $v = 42 / 0;
say 'It still works!';
```

However, as soon as the result stored in the $v variable is about to be displayed, the program stops execution with an error:

```
my $v = 42 / 0;
say $v;
```

The error message appears in the console:

```
Attempt to divide 42 by zero using div
  in block <unit> at divide0.rk line 2
```

The above-mentioned behaviour is called *soft failure*. It fails only if someone sees it :-) To catch the error, use the `try` and the `CATCH` blocks:

```
try {
    say 42 / 0;
    CATCH {
        default {
            say 'Error!';
        }
    }
}
say 'It still works!';
```

Random numbers

32. Generating random numbers

Generate a random number between 0 and N.

Use the `rand` method, which returns a random number between 0 and the value of its invocant:

```
say 1.rand;      # between 0 and 1
say 2.5.rand;    # between 0 and 2.5
say pi.rand;     # between 0 and 3.14...
```

The `rand` method is defined in the `Cool` class, which is the base class for the `Int`, `Num`, and `Rat` types. It always returns a floating-point value of the `Num` data type.

To generate random integer numbers, call the `Int` method:

```
say 10.rand.Int;  # Either 0, or 1, 2, 3, 4, 5, 6, 7, 8, or 9 but not 10
```

The `srand` function initializes the random numbers generator. The function expects an integer argument:

```
srand(1);
```

After setting the seed, the `rand` method starts generating numbers in the same sequence.

```
srand(1);
my $a = 10.rand;


srand(1);
my $b = 10.rand;


say $a == $b; # True
```

33. Neumann's random generator

Implement the von Neumann's random number generator (also known as Middle-square method).

This algorithm is a simple method of generating short sequences of four-digit random integers. The method has its drawbacks, but for us, it is an interesting algorithmic task. The recipe has these steps:

1. *Take a number between 0 and 9999.*
2. *Calculate the square of it.*
3. *If necessary, add leading zeros to make the number 8-digit.*
4. *Take the middle four digits.*
5. *Repeat from step 2.*

To illustrate it with an example, let's take the number 1234 as the seed. On step 2, it becomes 1522756; after step 3, 01522756. Finally, step 4 extracts the number 5227. Now we can implement it in code.

```
my $n = 1234;
$n **= 2;
$n = sprintf '%08i', $seed;
$n ~~ s/^..(.*)..$/$0/;
say $n;
```

Calculating the square of a number is done using the **= operator. This is a meta-operator based on the ** operator. The value is powered by two, and the result is assigned back to the variable.

It is possible to simplify the steps of taking the middle digits as there is actually no need of adding leading zeroes and asking the regex to always match eight characters. So, instead of capturing the number with /^..(.*)..$/, just take zero to four digits before the last two. If there are less than four digits, this is also fine because, in the original algorithm, the missing digits would be zeroes.

```
my $n = 1234;
$n **= 2;
$n ~~ /(. ** 0..4)..$/;
say ~$0;
```

We can also get rid of the regex replacement s/// and use the stringified value of the match object: ~$0.

Alternatively, instead of treating the number as a string, pure numeric manipulations may be done to achieve the same goal. Getting the middle four digits is possible using integer division and the modulo operation:

```
my $n = 1234;
$n **= 2;
$n = ($n / 100).Int % 10000;
say ~$0;
```

Whatever method you use, play around with the seed value and see how long the generator has been producing good-looking data.

```
my $n = 1234;
for 1..30 {
    $n **= 2;
    $n ~~ /(. ** 0..4)..$/;
    $n = ~$0;
    say $n;
}
```

Notice that in the loop, you need to update $n to use it in the next cycle.

In many cases, after some number of repetitions, the values converge to 0000. In some cases, such as with the initial number 2916, the period of the pseudorandom sequence is extremely short.

34. Histogram of random numbers

Test the quality of the random generator by using a histogram to visualise the distribution.

The quality of the built-in generator of random numbers fully depends on the algorithm the developers of the compiler used. As a user, you cannot do much to change the existing generator, but you can always test if it delivers numbers uniformly distributed across the whole interval.

There is the `rand` routine (see Task 32, *Generating random numbers*) that returns a floating-point number (actually, the value of the `Num` type) between 0 and 1. We will run it 100,000 times, filling the histogram containing 10 cells. Each random number falls into one of them. For example, the numbers between 0 and 0.1 land in the first cell, the numbers between 0.1 and 0.2 in the second, and so on.

```
my @histogram;
@histogram[10 * rand]++ for 1..100_000;
say @histogram;
```

Examine the way the index for the `@histogram` array is formed. A random integer between 0 and 1 is first multiplied by 10 and then an integer part of it is taken because the array indexing operator [ ] needs integers only. It is also possible to do the conversion explicitly:

```
@histogram[(10 * rand).Int]++
```

Run the program a few times. Here's the output of a couple of runs of the program, and it printed more or less equal numbers in each cell:

```
[10062 9818 10057 9922 10002 10118 9978 9959 10013 10071]
[9959 9957 9813 9933 10160 10030 10036 10032 10059 10021]
```

Mathematical problems

35. Distance between two points

Calculate the distance between the two points on a surface.

There are two points on a surface, each with their own coordinates, x and y. The task is to find the distance between these two points.

A straightforward solution would be to use the Pythagorean theorem:

```
my ($x1, $y1) = (10, 3);
my ($x2, $y2) = (9, 1);
say sqrt(($x1 - $x2) ** 2 + ($y1 - $y2) ** 2);
```

This works, but it requires a lot of typing. In Raku, there is a slightly easier way if you use complex numbers.

```
my $a = 10+3i;
my $b = 9+1i;
say ($a - $b).abs;
```

The result of both programs is the same. Complex numbers are objects of the `Complex` data type and are introduced via i—the imaginary unit:

The result of the difference `$a - $b` is also a complex number, and the `abs` method can be called on it. This method returns the absolute value of a complex number, which is actually the distance between the two points.

Notice the style: `10+3i` vs. `10 + 3i`. The first one seems to be preferable as it is also used as the default output format by the compiler. The second option may be confusing when a complex number is used in an expression with other variables or numbers.

```
$ raku -e'say (10+3i, -i, 4i, 10+0i)'
(10+3i -0-1i 0+4i 10+0i)
```

36. Standard deviation

For the given data, calculate the standard deviation value (sigma).

Standard deviation is a statistical term that shows how compact data distribution is. The formula is the following:

$$\sigma = \sqrt{\frac{\sum (x_i - \bar{x})^2}{N - 1}},$$

where N is the number of elements in the array x; $\bar{x}$ is the average value (see Task 56, *Average on an array*).

Let's use some test data from Wikipedia and take the straightforward approach using reduction operations and avoiding explicit loops:

```
my @data = 727.7, 1086.5, 1091.0, 1361.3, 1490.5, 1956.1;


my $avg = ([+] @data) / @data.elems;
my $sigma = sqrt(
    ([+] map * ** 2, map * - $avg, @data) /
    (@data.elems - 1)
);


say $sigma; # 420.962489619523
```

Inside the sqrt function, the [+] reduction operator gets the array that is formed by the two nested runs of map. First, the constant shift has been removed by applying * - $avg to each element. Second, a square of each item has been calculated: * ** 2.

In both cases, the WhateverCode is used. It is usually more expressive but may lead to constructs like * ** 2, which look a bit cryptic.

The two maps can be merged into one:

```
my $sigma = sqrt(
    ([+] map (* - $avg) ** 2, @data)  / (@data.elems - 1)
);
```

Now, let's explore the second approach that gets the same result using *feed operators*. In Raku, there are feed operators of both directions: <== and ==>. Their shape indicates the direction of data flow, so here is another version of the program.

```
my @data = 727.7, 1086.5, 1091.0, 1361.3, 1490.5, 1956.1;

my $avg = ([+] @data) / @data.elems;
@data
    ==> map * - $avg
    ==> map * ** 2
    ==> reduce * + *
    ==> my @σ;
say sqrt(@σ[0] / (@data.elems - 1)); # 420.962489619523
```

The data flow is clearly visible now. The @data array passes the two maps, and then, it is reduced using the + operation. The call of reduce * + * is equivalent to using the reduction operator in the form of [+].

Notice how the @σ array is defined, not only the fact that a Unicode name is used but mostly the fact that the my declaration is placed at the end of the feed chain. An array is used here because the feed operator does not return a scalar value, although we only need one element.

To make the code even closer to the original mathematical formula, you may choose a different name for the variable holding the average value (and remove the elems call):

```
my $x̄ = ([+] @data) / @data;
```

37. Polar coordinates

Convert the Cartesian coordinates to polar and backward.

Polar coordinates are a convenient way of representing points on a surface with the two values: distance from the centre of coordinates and the angle between the vector and the pole axis.

The conversion formulae between the Cartesian and polar systems, which is valid for positive x and y, are the following:

$$x = r \cos \varphi, \qquad y = r \sin \varphi;$$

$$r = \sqrt{x^2 + y^2}, \qquad \varphi = \arctan \frac{y}{x}.$$

These expressions can be implemented as-is in the code:

```
sub polar-to-cartesian($r, $φ) {
    $r * cos($φ), $r * sin($φ)
}

sub cartesian-to-polar($x, $y) {
    sqrt($x² + $y²), atan($y / $x)
}
```

The functions return lists of either polar or Cartesian coordinates. Because of the simplicity of implementation, it is fine to omit the `return` keyword and the semicolon at the end of the line.

Call the conversion functions with some positive numbers and check that the initial coordinates are restored after the second conversion:

```
say cartesian-to-polar(1, 2);
say polar-to-cartesian(2.236068, 1.107149);
```

For the negative x and y, the Cartesian-to-polar conversion is a bit more complicated. Depending on the quadrant of the point, the φ value is bigger or smaller by π. When x is zero, it is either $-\frac{\pi}{2}$ or $\frac{\pi}{2}$.

All these variants can be implemented by using multi-subroutines with the `where` clause, as demonstrated below:

```
sub cartesian-to-polar($x, $y) {
    sqrt($x² + $y²), cartesian-to-ϕ($x, $y)
}


multi sub cartesian-to-ϕ($x, $y where {$x > 0}) {
    atan($y / $x)
}


multi sub cartesian-to-ϕ($x, $y where {$x < 0 && $y ≥ 0}) {
    atan($y / $x) + π
}


multi sub cartesian-to-ϕ($x, $y where {$x < 0 && $y < 0}) {
    atan($y / $x) - π
}


multi sub cartesian-to-ϕ($x, $y where {$x == 0 && $y > 0}) {
    π / 2
}


multi sub cartesian-to-ϕ($x, $y where {$x == 0 && $y < 0}) {
    -π / 2
}


multi sub cartesian-to-ϕ($x, $y where {$x == 0 && $y == 0}) {
    Nil
}
```

38. Monte Carlo method

Calculate the area of a circle and the volume of a sphere of radius 1 using the Monte Carlo method.

The Monte Carlo method is a statistical method of calculating data whose formula is not known. The idea is to generate a big number of random numbers and see how many of them satisfy the condition.

To calculate the area of a circle of the radius 1, pairs of random numbers between -1 and 1 are generated. These pairs represent the points in the square in the center of coordinates with sides of length 2. The area of the square is thus 4. If the distance between the random point and the center of the square is less than 1, then this point is located inside the circle of that radius. Counting the number of points that landed inside the circle and the number of points outside the circle gives the approximate value of the area of the circle, as soon as the area of the square is known. Here is the program.

```
my $inside = 0;
my $n = 100_000;
for 1..$n {
    my @point = map {2.rand - 1}, 1..2; # 1..3 for sphere
    $inside++ if sqrt([+] map *², @point) < 1;
}
say 4 * $inside / $n;                    # 8 for sphere
```

The bigger the number of repetitions $n, the more accurate is the result. In one of the runs of the program, it printed `3.14392`, which is close to the true result, which is πr^2, which is equal to π in our case. We see that the Monte Carlo result is very close.

For the volume of a sphere, change the program according to the comments. The formula is $\frac{4}{3}\pi r^3$, which approximately gives `4.189`.

2.4

Numbers and strings

39. Unicode digits

Print all Unicode digits.

Raku has the best support of Unicode among the modern programming languages. When talking about digits, it is worth remembering that the Unicode standard marks as digits much more than the regular ten characters used in English, for example.

Let us iterate over the whole range of codepoints and select the digits using the `<:digit>` character class in the regex.

```
for 1 .. 0x10FFFD {
    my $char = $_.chr;
    print $char if $char ~~ /<:digit>/;
}
```

The program prints 580 characters. Let us list some of them:

0123456789・١٢٢٤٥٦٧٧٨٩・١٢٢٤٥٦٧٨٩□□□□□□□□□□□□٠۱۲۳۴۵۶۷۸۹०१२
०८৫৬৭৮৯০੧੨੩੪੫੬੭੮੯੦૧૨૩૪ ૫૬૭૮૯ ୦୧୨୩ ୪୫୬୭୮୯ ୦க௨ ௩ச ௫௬௭௮௯ அ
க௧௦௩௨௩௪௫௬௭௮௯௦௧ ௨௩ ௪௫௬௭௮ ௦ ౦౧ ౨౩౪ ౫ ౬౭ ౮౯ ౦౧౨౩౪౫ ౬౭౮౯౦
೧೨೩೪ ೫೬೭೮೯ ೦ ೧೨೩೪೫೬೭೮೯ ൦ ൧൨൩൪൫൬൭൮൯ ෦෧෨෩෪෫෬෭෮෯ 0

 1 2 3 4 5 6 7 8 9
01234567890123456789**0123456789****0123456789**0123456789

If you want to know the name of the Unicode digit, call the uniname method on the character:

```
say $char ~ ' ' ~ $char.uniname if $char ~~ /<:digit>/;
```

For example, Arabic digits 0 to 9 have simple names such as DIGIT ZERO;
another set of Arabic digits ٠, ١, ٢, etc., up to ٩ has names such as ARABIC-
INDIC DIGIT THREE.

40. Guess the number

Write a program that generates a random integer number 0 through 10 and asks the user to guess it, saying if the entered value is too small or too big.

First, a random number needs to be generated. In Raku, the `rand` routine can be called on an integer object, and it returns a random floating-point value between 0 and that integer. As the task requires a random integer number, call the `round` method on the result:

```
10.rand.round
```

Now, ask for the initial guess and enter the loop, which compares the guess with $n.

```
my $n = 10.rand.round;

my $guess = prompt('Guess my number between 0 and 10: ');

while $guess != $n {
    if $guess < $n {
        say 'Too small.';
    }
    elsif $guess > $n {
        say 'Too big.';
    }
    $guess = prompt('Try again: ');
}

say 'Yes, this is it!';
```

The `if-elsif` chain may be replaced with a ternary operator:

```
say $guess < $n ?? 'Too small.' !! 'Too big.';
```

41. Binary to integer

Convert a binary number to a decimal integer.

Raku is good at its ease of switching between numerical and string representation of the same data. This task is an example where this feature can be used.

The idea is to take a binary number, treat it as a string, prepend the `0b` prefix indicating the binary value, and convert the value back to the integer, but a decimal this time. This description is encoded in the following example:

```
my $bin = '101101';
my $int = "0b$bin".Int;
say $int;
```

This program prints `45`.

It is possible to use an alternative representation of the binary number using a generic form of the value with an explicit radix:

```
my $bin = '101101';
my $int = ":2<$bin>".Int;
say $int;
```

As a side note, remember that you cannot start a numeric literal with 0. For example, the following assignment is incorrect:

```
my $b = 0110;
```

This generates a compile-time error, saying that the leading 0 no longer means octal numbers. In Raku, all the radix prefixes are unified: `0b` for binary, `0x` for hexadecimal, and `0o` for octal representation.

42. Integer as binary, octal, and hex

Print a given integer number in the binary, octal, and hexadecimal represen-
tations.

On an integer object, call the `base` method with the corresponding number:

```
say 42.base(2);  # 101010
say 42.base(8);  # 52
say 42.base(16); # 2A
```

Alternatively, use the `fmt` method, which is defined for integers and accepts
the formatting string in the `printf` format:

```
my $int = 42;
say $int.fmt('Hex: %x'); # Hex: 2a
say $int.fmt('Oct: %o'); # Oct: 52
say $int.fmt('Bin: %b'); # Bin: 101010
```

There also exists a conventional function `printf`, which works similarly to
how it behaves in other programming languages: It needs a formatting string
and a list of values to be substituted to the %-placeholders.

```
my $int = 42;
printf("Hex: %x\n", $int); # Hex: 2a
printf("Oct: %o\n", $int); # Oct: 52
printf("Bin: %b\n", $int); # Bin: 101010
```

The above examples print the values without their radix prefixes. To add a
prefix, use the %# forms:

```
printf("Hex: %#x\n", $int); # Hex: 0x2a
printf("Oct: %#o\n", $int); # Oct: 052 (not 0o52!)
printf("Bin: %#b\n", $int); # Bin: 0b101010
```

43. Sum of digits

Calculate the sum of digits of a given number.

The solution of this task is based on the `split` method that you can call on any object that is convertible to strings.

The following code takes an integer number and splits it into separate characters, one per digit. Then the reduction operator adds up all the digits, and the result is printed.

```
my $number = 139487854;
say [+] $number.split('');
```

The conversion of an integer to a string happens at the moment the `split` method is called. The resulting array contains a number of one-character elements. When they are passed to the [+] operator, which expects numeric data, characters are converted back to numbers so that they can be added up as numbers, not strings.

Compare the presented solution with a straightforward approach, where the given number is treated as a number, and a series of divisions has to be performed to get separate digits:

```
my $number = 139487854;
my $sum = 0;

while ($number) {
    $sum += $number % 10;
    $number = Int($number / 10);
}
say $sum; # Still prints 49
```

44. Bit counter

Count the number of bits set to 1 in a binary representation of a positive integer number.

There are two approaches to this task: either treat the binary sequence as a string or count real bits in the machine representation of the number. Both approaches are fine. We restrict ourselves to the positive integers to avoid dealing with two's complements representations.

First, use textual approach.

```
my $value = prompt('Enter value > ');
$value = $value.Int.base(2);
say "Binary representation: $value";
$value ~~ s:g/0//;
say "Number of 1s: {$value.chars}";
```

The entered value gets converted to a string containing binary representation (see also Task 42, *Integer as binary, octal, and hex*). Then, all the zeros are removed from the string using the regex substitution:

```
$value ~~ s:g/0//;
```

At this point, the `$value` string contains only set bits, so the length of the string is the number of such bits. To get the length of the string, call the `chars` method (see Task 3, *String length*).

Run the program:

```
$ raku bit-count.rk
Enter value > 12345
Binary representation: 11000000111001
Number of 1s: 6
```

Now, the other approach works directly with bits.

```
my $value = prompt('Enter value > ');

my $bits = 0;
repeat {
    $bits++ if $value +& 1;
    $value = $value +> 1;
} while $value > 0;

say "Number of 1s: $bits";
```

This program uses two bitwise operators. They are prefixed with +: +& for
the binary AND operation and +> for the binary shift.

In the `repeat ... while` loop, the value is tested for the presence of 1 in the
lowest bit: `if $value +& 1`. If this bit is set, the `$bits` counter is incremented.

Then, the `$value` is shifted to the right by one bit (which is equivalent to
dividing it by two). The loop is over when the `$value` becomes zero, in other
words, when all the bits are shifted out.

Notice that the `$value` variable is seamlessly used first as a string (after re-
turning from the `prompt` routine), and then as an integer.

Test the program with the same input value as in the first example:

```
$ raku bit-count2.rk
Enter value > 12345
Number of 1s: 6
```

If there are no performance demands, the first approach using texts seems
to be more natural for Raku; however, if you need higher performance, consider pre-calculating the number of bits and saving it in an array.

45. Compose the largest number

Given the list of integers, compose the largest possible number by concatenating them.

This task requires working with the same data as with numbers and strings. To compose the largest possible number out of a list of integers, we need to reorder them so that the largest numbers come first.

The easiest way to achieve that is to treat numbers as strings, sort them alphabetically in descending order, concatenate the pieces to a single string, and get the resulting integer.

```
my @a = (67, 8, 1, 5, 45);

say @a.sort({$^b.Str cmp $^a.Str}).join;
```

Sorting an array is achieved by the `sort` method, which optionally takes the code block that is used in comparison:

```
{$^b.Str cmp $^a.Str}
```

The two special variables, `$^a` and `$^b`, are the so-called *placeholders* that get the values of the arguments passed to the code block. The order of the arguments corresponds to the alphabetical order of the variables. It can be either `$^a` and `$^b` or `$^x` and `$^y` or even `$^arg1` and `$^arg2`. As the goal is to sort strings in descending order, `$b` is mentioned first in comparison.

During the sorting procedure, `$^a` and `$^b` are referencing to different elements of the given array. The `cmp` operator is the universal comparison operator. To make sure the arguments are sorted alphabetically, they are both casted to strings by calling the `Str` method.

The result of running the program is `8675451`.

46. Convert to Roman numerals

Convert an integer number to a Roman numerals string.

Roman numbers are not a direct translation of the decimal system. In this task, we assume that the number is not more than 3999, which is the maximum a regular Roman number can reach.

Let's use the algorithm that keeps the table of pre-calculated sequences of Roman letters so that we don't have to check when III becomes IV, or when another I appears after V, etc.

In the program below, there are four such sequences: for thousands, hundreds, tens, and ones. The program iterates over the digits of the number in the decimal representation and chooses one of the values from the array of lists stored in the @roman variable.

```
my $n = 2018;

my $roman;
my @roman =
    1000 => < M MM MMM >,
    100  => < C CC CCC CD D DC DCC DCCC CM >,
    10   => < X XX XXX XL L LX LXX LXXX XC >,
    1    => < I II III IV V VI VII VIII IX >;

for @roman -> $x {
    my $digit = ($n / $x.key).Int;
    $roman ~= $x.value[$digit - 1] if $digit;
    $n %= $x.key;
}

say $roman; # MMXVIII
```

Let us examine the structure of the @roman container. In the program code, it looks like a hash. Indeed, it could be a hash, but in our case, the algorithm requires division by 1000, 100, and 10, so it is easier to organise data so that they are already sorted in the correct order.

The < > quotation construct in the program is the simplest way to create a list from the strings that do not contain spaces. If you print it with the say @roman instruction, you'll get the following:

```
[1000 => (M MM MMM) 100 => (C CC CCC CD D DC DCC DCCC CM) 10
=> (X XX XXX XL L LX LXX LXXX XC) 1 => (I II III IV V VI VII
VIII IX)]
```

On the top level, it is a list of pairs, such as 1000 => (M MM MMM). Pairs, or objects of the Pair class, have the key and value methods. For the shown example of a pair, the key method returns 1000, and the value method returns a list (M MM MMM).

The digits of the input number $n are scanned from left to right:

```
my $digit = ($n / $x.key).Int;
```

The value of $n also becomes smaller and smaller at each step:

```
$n %= $x.key;
```

At each iteration, the next digit lands in the $digit variable, and it is used as the index that selects the correct Roman representation:

```
$roman ~= $x.value[$digit - 1] if $digit;
```

As zeros in the decimal form have no correspondence to the Roman numbers, only non-zero values are taken. When the loop is over, the $roman variable contains the desired Roman string.

The opposite conversion is examined in Task 84, *Decode Roman numerals*.

47. Spelling numbers

Write an integer number below one million in words.

Human languages have many inconsistencies, especially in the most frequent constructs. Spelling numbers seems to be a simple task, but due to a number of small differences, the resulting program is quite big.

The program is listed on the next page. Let's discuss the algorithm first.

Take a number; for example, *987,654*. The rules for spelling out the groups of three digits, *987* and *654*, are the same. For the first group, the word *thousand* must be added.

Now, examine a group of three digits. The first digit is the number of hundreds, and it has to be spelled only if it is not zero. If it is not zero, then we spell the digit and add the word *hundred*.

Now, remove the leftmost digit, and we've got two digits left. If the remaining two digits form the number from 1 to 20, then it can be directly converted to the corresponding name. The names for the numbers from 0 to 10 are obviously different. The names for the numbers from 11 to 19 have some commonalities, but is it still easier to directly prepare the names for all of them.

For the larger numbers (21 to 99), there are two cases. If the number is dividable by 10 then a name for 20, 30, 40, etc. is taken. If not, then the name is built of the name of tens and the name for units, joined with a hyphen, such as *forty-five*.

The *zero* name appears only in the case when the given number is zero.

In the program, the names are listed in the `@names` array. The `if—elsif—else` chain implements the above-described procedure.

```
my @names = <zero one two three four five six seven eight
             nine ten eleven twelve thirteen fourteen fifteen
             sixteen seventeen eighteen nineteen twenty
             thirty forty fifty sixty seventy eighty ninety>;

sub spell-number($number) {
    my $n = $number.Int;

    my $r;
    if $n < 20 {
        $r = @names[$n];
    }
    elsif $n < 100 {
        $r = @names[$n / 10 + 18];
        $r ~= '-' ~ @names[$n % 10] if $n % 10;
    }
    elsif $n < 1000 {
        $r = @names[$n / 100] ~ ' hundred';
        $r ~= ' ' ~ spell-number($n % 100) if $n % 100;
    }
    else {
        $r = spell-number($n / 1000) ~ ' thousand';
        $r ~= ' ' ~ spell-number($n % 1000) if $n % 1000;
    }

    return $r;
}
```

Try running the program with a few different numbers:

```
say spell-number(987654);    # nine hundred eighty-seven
                             # thousand six hundred fifty-four
say spell-number(0);         # zero
say spell-number(17);        # seventeen
say spell-number(100_001);   # one hundred thousand one
```

All work well, but you can do it differently with the help of multi-subs. In the next version of the program, the chain of the checks is replaced with the same number of subroutines that know with what numbers they can work best. The common part is extracted to a separate sub `spell-part`.

```
my @names = <zero one two three four five six seven eight
             nine ten eleven twelve thirteen fourteen fifteen
             sixteen seventeen eighteen nineteen twenty
             thirty forty fifty sixty seventy eighty ninety>;

multi sub spell-number(Int $n where {$n < 20}) {
    return @names[$n];
}

multi sub spell-number(Int $n where {$n < 100}) {
    my $r = @names[$n / 10 + 18];
    $r ~= '-' ~ @names[$n % 10] if $n % 10;
    return $r;
}

multi sub spell-number(Int $n where {$n < 1000}) {
    return spell-part($n, 100, 'hundred');
}

multi sub spell-number(Int $n where {$n < 1_000_000}) {
    return spell-part($n, 1000, 'thousand');
}

sub spell-part(Int $n, Int $base, Str $name) {
    my $r = spell-number(($n / $base).Int) ~ ' ' ~ $name;
    $r ~= ' ' ~ spell-number($n % $base) if $n % $base;
    return $r;
}
```

Modify the program to process numbers greater than a million.

Chapter 3

Aggregate Data Types

Manipulating lists and arrays

48. Swap two values

Swap the values of two variables.

In Raku, there is no need to use temporary variables to swap the values of two variables. Just use the lists on both sides of the equation:

```
($b, $a) = ($a, $b);
```

Alternatively, call the `reverse` method and assign the result back to the values:

```
($a, $b).=reverse;
```

Consider the complete program:

```
my ($a, $b) = (10, 20);
($b, $a) = ($a, $b);
say "\$a = $a, \$b = $b";
```

This program prints the swapped values:

```
$a = 20, $b = 10
```

This approach also works with elements of an array:

```
my @a = (3, 5, 7, 4);
(@a[2], @a[3]) = (@a[3], @a[2]);
say @a; # [3 5 4 7]
```

A slice of an array may be used instead of an explicit list:

```
my @a = (3, 5, 7, 4);
@a[1, 2] = @a[2, 1];
say @a; # [3 7 5 4]
```

49. Reverse a list

Print the given list in reverse order.

Start with an array of integer numbers.

```
my @a = (10, 20, 30, 40, 50);
```

To reverse the array, call the `reverse` method on it.

```
say @a.reverse;
```

This line prints the required result:

```
(50 40 30 20 10)
```

Notice that the initial array stays unchanged. The `reverse` method creates a new sequence and returns it.

The same method works with other types of data that can be converted to a sequence, for example, ranges.

Print a range in reversed order:

```
my $range = 10..15;
say $range;
say $range.reverse;
```

Again, the original range is not changed, and the returned value is not a range but a sequence. Compare the results of printing an original value of $range with what the `reverse` method returns:

```
10..15
(15 14 13 12 11 10)
```

50. Rotate a list

Move all elements of an array N positions to the left or to the right.

Array is a data type in Raku that offers the rotate method, which does exactly what is needed. It takes an argument that tells the length and direction of the rotation.

```
my @a = (1, 3, 5, 7, 9, 11, 13, 15);

say @a.rotate(3);
say @a.rotate(-3);
```

Positive values rotate to the left; negative values rotate to the right. Elements that go beyond the array borders, are appended to the end (or to the beginning if rotating to the right).

The original array stays untouched. The program prints the following:

```
[7 9 11 13 15 1 3 5]
[11 13 15 1 3 5 7 9]
```

To modify the array, assign the result of rotation to the variable itself:

```
@a.=rotate(3);
```

Alternatively, a pair of shift and push methods can lead to the same result:

```
@a.push(@a.shift) for 1..3;
```

Rotating to the opposite side can be done using complementary methods:

```
@a.unshift(@a.pop) for 1..3;
```

In the last three examples, @a is updated after the operations.

51. Randomise an array

Shuffle the elements of an array in random order.

Arrays in Raku have the `pick` method, which does the work.

```
my @a = 1..20;
say @a.pick(@a);
```

A possible output of the program looks like this:

```
(4 18 10 15 14 8 2 11 3 12 1 6 9 19 13 7 16 17 20 5)
```

The `pick` method expects an integer argument that defines the number of picked elements. In the example above, passing the array as an argument causes the language to coerce it into an integer by calling the `@a.Int` method, which returns the length of the array.

After the operation, the original data remains unchanged. If you need to update the `@a` variable, use the `.=` operator to call a method and assign its result to the invocant:

```
@a.=pick(@a);
```

Elements of the array are not repeated in the output.

Arrays also have the `roll` method, which works similar but does not guarantee that the elements are not repeated.

```
say @a.roll(@a);
```

Calling either `pick` or `roll` with no argument returns a single element from an array. If the value of the argument is bigger than the length of the array, the `pick` method returns the list of the same size as the original one, while `roll` happily generates more repeated items.

52. Incrementing array elements

Increment each element in an array.

In Raku, there is no need to explicitly iterate over an array to apply some operation to each element. Use a hyper-operator:

```
@data>>++;
```

Let us try it on a small array:

```
my @data = 1..10;
@data>>++;
say @data; #[2 3 4 5 6 7 8 9 10 11]
```

The >>++ operator is a hyper-operator that applies the ++ operator to each element of the array. As the ++ operator modifies the element, the whole @data array is also modified after the operation.

Alternatively, one of the following forms may be used:

```
@data <<+=>> 1;
@data >>+=>> 1;
```

These constructions take every element of the array and perform the += 1 operation on it.

Notice that if you omit the = sign in the last examples, the original data is not modified.

```
my @data = 1..10;
my @new-data = @data >>+>> 1;
say @data;     #[1 2 3 4 5 6 7 8 9 10]
say @new-data; #[2 3 4 5 6 7 8 9 10 11]
```

53. Adding up two arrays

Take two arrays and create a new one whose elements are the sums of the corresponding items of the initial arrays.

At first, we assume that the arrays are of the same length. In this case, the easiest way to solve the task is to use a meta-operator:

```
my @a = 10..20;
my @b = 30..40;

my @sum = @a <<+>> @b;
say @sum; # [40 42 44 46 48 50 52 54 56 58 60]
```

Meta-operators may take a few different forms. In the case of the + operator, it is possible to construct the following meta-operators and their alternatives using the Unicode characters:

```
<<+>>        «+»
>>+<<        »+«
>>+>>        »+»
<<+<<        «+«
```

For the above arrays of the same length, all the operators work the same. The difference between them becomes important when the operands are arrays with different numbers of elements. The sharp angles of the arrows must be directed toward the shorter operand.

You can memorise that rule by comparing the operator with the 'more' and 'less' operators > and <. The longer array stands at the 'bigger' end. Depending on the operator, the shorter array is either repeated as many times as needed to make pairs of each element of the longer array or is only connected with the first few elements of it. Otherwise, an exception occurs.

Consider the following four combinations with arrays of different lengths:

```
my @long = 1, 2, 3, 4;
my @short = 10, 20;

@long <<+<< @short;
@long >>+>> @short;
@long <<+>> @short;
@long >>+<< @short;
```

The first three additions compile and run:

```
say @long <<+<< @short; # [11 22]
say @long >>+>> @short; # [11 22 13 24]
say @long <<+>> @short; # [11 22 13 24]
```

As you see, the `<<+<<` operator only addresses the first two elements of the four-element array.

The `>>+>>` operator repeats the short array twice, and the four values [10, 20, 10, 20] add up to the four values of the `@long` array.

The most tolerant operator is `<<+>>`. It lets the operands have different lengths and makes the shorter one longer if necessary.

The `>>+<<` operator requires both operands to have the same length. So, in our example, a runtime error is generated. This operator is called *non-dwimmy* in the error message because it does not try to adjust to your needs.

```
Lists on either side of non-dwimmy hyperop of infix:<+> are
not of the same length
left: 4 elements, right: 2 elements
```

You have to decide whether or not you are going to use the Unicode forms of the operators.

54. Exclusion of two arrays

From the given two arrays, find the elements of the first array which do not appear in the second one.

Take two arbitrary arrays of integers:

```
my @a = 2, 5, 7, 8, 10;
my @b = 1, 3, 5, 7, 9;
```

The program should print 2, 8, and 10. Here is a possible solution:

```
.say for (@a \ @b).keys;
```

Notice that the \ infix operator is a Unicode character, not an ASCII back-slash. Most likely, it is better to avoid using it in favour of its ASCII replacement:

```
.say for (@a (-) @b).keys;
```

In these examples, the arrays are converted to sets before the operation.

Sets do not keep the order, thus if you need to preserve the order, you can do it differently:

```
.say for grep * ∉ @b, @a;
```

The `grep` function gets a `WhateverCode` block * ∉ $b, which is equivalent to the block with the default variable: {$_ ∉ $b}.

The ∉ operator returns `True` if its first operand, being treated as a set, is contained within the set on the right-hand side. The operator can be spelled purely in ASCII:

```
.say for grep * !(<) $b, @a;
```

3.2

Information retrieval

55. Sum of the elements of an array

Find the sum of the elements of an array of integers.

There is an array of integers:

```
my @a = (4, 6, 8, 1, 0, 58, 1, 34, 7, 4, 2);
```

There is no need to explicitly iterate over the elements to calculate the sum of its elements. Rather use the reduction operator:

```
say [+] @a;
```

Any reduction operator takes a list of values and inserts the actual operator between them.

For example, to get the sum of all the elements that are greater than 10, grep the initial array and apply [+] to it:

```
say [+] grep {$_ > 10}, @a; # Prints 92
```

If you prefer more unreadable syntax, the reduction operation can be spelled down wordier:

```
say reduce &infix:<+>, @a; # Prints 125
```

This gives the same result as say [+] @a, which is the better choice in most cases.

Here's another simple solution using the sum method:

```
my @a = (4, 6, 8, 1, 0, 58, 1, 34, 7, 4, 2);
say @a.sum(); # Also 125
```

Chose whatever approach you like the most.

56. Average of an array

Find the average value of the given array of numbers.

Calculating the average value of an array has two subtasks—calculate the sum and divide it by the size of the array. So, one of the solutions can look like this:

```
my @data = 7, 11, 34, 50, 200;
say sum(@data) / @data;
```

Here, the `sum` built-in function returns the sum of the elements of the `@data` array. To get the size of an array, you may call the `elems` method:

```
say sum(@data) / @data.elems;
```

This is a straightforward way, which is a bit redundant for our task. As the `@data` is used in numeric context as an operand of the division operator, explicitly calling the `elems` method is not necessary.

Another approach is to use the reduction operator:

```
say ([+] @data) / @data;
```

In this example, `[+] @data` is equivalent to `@data[0] + @data[1] + ... + @data[N]`, where the `+` operator is placed between all the elements of the array.

Be careful with the parentheses in this code. If you omit them, the result will be incorrect, as the actual sum consists of a single element `@data / @data`, which equals one. If you omit the space before the opening brace, it will be considered as a parenthesis grouping the arguments of the `say` function, and the result is also incorrect, as the code prints only the sum of the array elements and divides the result of `say` (which is 1).

57. Moving average

Calculate the moving average for the given array of numbers.

For each element of an array, the moving average is the average value of the last few items or the few elements around it. This kind of analysis is often used to smooth the curve.

Let us first generate some random data—an array of a hundred values between 0 and 1:

```
my @data = map {rand}, 1..100;
```

Now, calculate the average values for (almost) each point using three items before and three items after the current item:

```
my @average = map {
    sum(@data[$_ - 3 .. $_ + 3]) / 7
}, 3..96;
```

The beginning and the end of an initial array do not have enough neighbouring elements; that's why they are skipped.

Inside the `map` function, the code block calculates the sum of an array slice: `sum(@data[$_ - 3 .. $_ + 3])`.

Here is a graph with the results of a test run of this program. The inner curve corresponds to the values of the `@average` array.

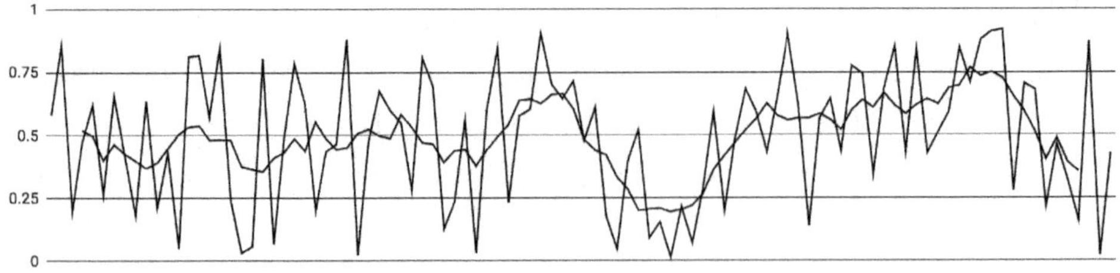

58. Is an element in a list?

Tell if the given value is in the list.

There are a few approaches to the problem. The most compact one seems to be the use of the *smartmatch* ~~ operator in combination with the any function:

```
my @array = (10, 14, 0, 15, 17, 20, 30, 35);
my $x = 17;
say 'In the list' if $x ~~ any @array;
```

To check if a given value is contained among the elements of an array or a list, use the grep routine.

```
say 'In the list' if grep $x, @array;
```

The grep routine returns a list of all the matched elements. In the Boolean context, the return value is True if at least one element was found. In the opposite case, an empty list coerces to False. If the element in question is not zero, then the first routine may be used instead of grep. It returns the first element that matches the search pattern:

```
say 'In the list' if first $x, @array;
```

To extend this to zero values, test the values before making a decision:

```
say 'In the list' if $x == first $x, @array;
```

Another solution is to convert the array to a hash and check if there is a key with the given value. This is useful when you need more than one check.

```
my %hash = map {$_ => 1}, @array;
say 'In the list' if %hash{$n};
```

59. First odd number

Find the first odd number in a list of integers.

The task is to find the first odd number in a given list of odd and even numbers. A good candidate is the `first` routine, which searches for the leftmost value (see, for example, Task 58, *Is an element in a list?*). Now, we can pass an anonymous code block to it to calculate the predicate.

```
my @nums = (2, 4, 18, 9, 16, 7, 10);
my $first = @nums.first: * % 2;
say $first; # Prints 9
```

Colon syntax is used here to pass arguments to methods. The same call may be written in the traditional style with parentheses:

```
my $first = @nums.first(* % 2);
```

The construction with a star (which is called *Whatever*) creates a code block with one argument, equivalent to `{$a % 2}`, that returns `True` when the number is odd. The same code can be rewritten less efficiently with a `grep`:

```
my @odd = grep {$_ % 2}, @nums;
say @odd[0]; # Prints 9
```

Let us try another method by matching the value against a regex that tests whether the last digit of a number is odd:

```
@nums ~~ /(\d*<[13579]>$)/;
say $/[0];
```

The whole array is matched against the regex, and the first captured value is printed.

60. Take every second element

Form a new array by picking every second element from the original array.

There is an array of numbers, and the task is to pick every second element and put them into a new array.

Prepare the test data:

```
my @data = 20..30;
```

Here is a possible solution:

```
my @selected = @data[1, 3 ... *];
say @selected;
```

This program prints the following values:

```
[21 23 25 27 29]
```

We are using a slice to provide the needed indices within the pair of square brackets. To make a slice, just list more than one element inside the brackets, for example:

```
say @data[2, 3, 5]; # (22 23 25)
```

To select every second element, a sequence `1, 3 ... *` is created. The `...` sequence operator creates a sequence based on the example list provided on its left side. The two numbers, 1 and 3, provide a pattern for the arithmetic progression; thus, every element is calculated as $x_n = x_{n-1} + 2$.

The star at the right end of the sequence ensures that the sequence is generated until the whole array has been looked up. Using the `*` is a very nice way to ask the compiler to do the right job for you (the *Do What I Mean*, or DWIM, principle).

61. Number of occurrences in array

Count how many times a particular element appears in the array.

Let's have an array with a list of fruits; some of them are repeated.

```
my @data = <
    apple       pear        grape       lemon
    peach       apple       banana      grape
    pineapple   avocado
>;
```

Now, the task is to count how many times the element `'grape'` appears there. First, extract all the elements to a temporary array by using the `grep` method, and then call the `elems` method to get the number of elements in the filtered data.

```
my $n = @data.grep('grape').elems;
say $n; # 2
```

Notice also a very handy way of defining arrays of strings. Instead of quoting all the elements, use the `<...>` syntax to create a list out of space-separated values.

If you need to determine the number of occurrences for more than one element, then it is better to use the more efficient technique to avoid `grepping` the array for every item.

```
my %count;
%count{$_}++ for @data;

say %count<pineapple>; # 1
say %count<grape>;     # 2
```

62. Finding unique elements

Print all unique elements of the given array.

Objects of the `Array` type have the `unique` method.

```
my @a = 2, 3, 7, 4, 5, 5, 6, 2, 10, 7;
say @a.unique;
```

The result of running this program is a sequence containing the unique elements: (2 3 7 4 5 6 10).

Notice that the values are not sorted and appear in the same order as they first appeared in the original data, which stays unchanged.

The routine can be used as a function:

```
say unique(@a);
```

It can also take a code block or a reference passed via the `with` named argument to replace the default comparison method. The following example demonstrates how to select rational numbers that only repeat once within the given integer part.

```
<1.1 1.3 2.2 2.5 3.6>.unique(with => {
    $^a.Int == $^b.Int;
}).say;
```

From the given list of numbers, only three pass the filter: (1.1 2.2 3.6).

The `$^a` and `$^b` are the placeholder variables that receive pairs of values when the `with` code block is activated. Alternatively, arguments with explicit names may be used:

```
unique(@data, with => -> $x, $y {$x.Int == $y.Int}).say;
```

63. Minimum and maximum

Find the minimum and the maximum numbers in the given list of integers.

Finding the minimum and maximum elements of arrays is extremely easy.
For *iterable* objects, the two methods, min and max, are defined.

```
my @list = 7, 6, 12, 3, 4, 10, 2, 5, 15, 6, 7, 8, 9, 3;

say @list.min;
say @list.max;
```

For the list in the example, this program prints two numbers:

```
2
15
```

The min and max routines can be used as binary operators, in which case they
return the smaller or the bigger number:

```
say 7 min 8; # Prints 7
say 7 max 8; # Prints 8
```

Operators can be chained like this:

```
say 7 min 5 min 8; # Prints 5
say 7 max 5 max 8; # Prints 8
```

This can be expressed with the help of a reduction meta-operator [...]:

```
say [min] 7, 9, 5; # Prints 5
say [max] 7, 9, 4; # Prints 9
```

Lists are also accepted, for example: say [min] @list.

64. Increasing sequences

Check if the given array contains increasing (or decreasing) numbers.

Given the list of numbers in an array, the task is to tell if all of them are sorted in ascending or descending order.

Take an array:

```
my @data = 3, 7, 19, 20, 34;
```

The reduction operators offer a very expressive and simple way to find the answer in one go:

```
say [<] @data;
```

With the values listed above, this program prints `True`. Change the array to break the increasing sequence, and the program prints `False`.

You will not be surprised to find out that to check whether the array is sorted in decreasing order, the code is as follows:

```
say [>] @data;
```

Using reduction operators is equivalent to inserting the main operator between the elements of the array, so `[<] @data` is the same as the following chain of comparison operations:

```
say @data[0] < @data[1] < @data[2] < @data[3] < @data[4];
```

By the way, Raku's ability to understand chained operations is very handy in the `if` conditions, for example:

```
my $x = 15;
say 'ok' if 10 < $x < 20;
```

Working with subroutines

65. Passing arrays to subroutines

Pass data, contained in an array, to a subroutine.

An array can be passed to a subroutine as easily as a scalar can. You simply define it in a signature and pass it together with other arguments.

```
my @colours = <red green blue>;


sub f(@data, $sep) {
    @data.join($sep).say;
}


f(@colours, ', ');  # Prints: red, green, blue
```

The `@colours` array is passed to the `f` sub, and it lands in the `@data` variable inside the sub. An additional second argument, `$sep`, receives its own data.

In cases when a sub expects separate scalars, and you've got your data in an array, flattening it helps:

```
sub g($a, $b, $c, $sep) {
    say "$a$sep$b$sep$c";
}
g(|@colours, ', ');  # Prints: red, green, blue
```

In the sub call, an array name is prefixed with a vertical bar, and the compiler, therefore, knows that you are not passing an array as a whole but that you are using its elements as values to be assigned to the scalar arguments `$a`, `$b`, and `$c`.

The number of elements in the array has to match with the number of corresponding subroutine arguments, otherwise one of the following errors occurs: `Too few positionals passed` or `Too many positionals passed`.

66. Variadic parameters in a sub

Pass a few scalars to a sub and work with them as with an array inside the sub.

The task is to take a few scalar parameters and pass them to a single array in the subroutine.

Here is an example of how to do that, prefixing an array name with a star:

```
sub h($sep, *@data) {
    @data.join($sep).say;
}

h(', ', 'red', 'green', 'blue');
```

The *@data struct is called a *slurpy* parameter. It is an array that consumes all of the arguments passed to the function after the $sep argument. In the example above, three string values are passed. It is also possible to pass any other number of arguments:

```
h(', ', 'apple');

h(', ', 1, 2, 3, 4, 5);
```

Or even as a range of values, all of which land in the @data array.

```
h(', ', 'a' .. 'z');
```

It is important that in comparison to the solutions from Task 65, *Passing arrays to subroutines*, the $sep argument is mentioned first in the sub signature. If you put it at the end, the compiler refuses to accept that and complains:

```
Cannot put required parameter $sep after variadic parameters
```

3.4

Multi-dimensional data

67. Transpose a matrix

Take a matrix and print its transposed version.

A matrix can be represented by nested arrays or lists. For example, here's a square 2×2 matrix:

```
my @matrix = [1, 2],
             [3, 4];
```

This is how the transposed matrix should look:

```
[[1, 3],
 [2, 4]]
```

Actually, the outer pair of square brackets, could be added to the initializer of the @matrix variable. Raku simply converts the list ([1, 2], [3, 4]) to an array when assigning it to an array variable @matrix.

Transposing a matrix is extremely easy:

```
my @transposed = [Z] @matrix;
```

The [Z] operator is a reduction form of the zip operator. For the given small matrix, it's action is equivalent to the following code:

```
my @transposed = [1, 2] Z [3, 4];
```

Despite the simplicity of the method, it works well with bigger matrices as well as non-square ones.

For the example @matrix in this task, the output of the program is the following:

```
[(1 3) (2 4)]
```

68. Sort hashes by parameter

Sort a list of hashes using data in their values.

This task is commonly performed to sort items where the sortable parameter
is one of the values in the hash, for example, sorting a list of people by age.

```
my @people = (
    {
        name => 'Kevin', age => 20,
    },
    . . .
    {
        name => 'Amanda', age => 19,
    },
);


@people.sort( *<age> ).say;
```

Using *<age> is the same as {%^a<age> <=> %^b<age>}.

The sort method uses an optional code block that customises the sorting
procedure. It takes two arguments, compares them, and returns the result
of the comparison.

In the example shown, %^a and %^b are the two placeholder variables created
by the compiler. They alphabetically correspond to the first and the second
arguments that the block receives.

Alternatively, it is possible to list the arguments in a pointy block explicitly:

```
@people.sort( -> %first, %second {
    %first<age> <=> %second<age>
}).say;
```

69. Count hash values

Having a hash, count the number of occurrences of each of its values.

For example, a hash is a collection mapping a car's license plate to the colour
of the car or a passport number to the name of the street where the person
lives. In the first example, the task is to count how many cars of each colour
there are. In the second example, we have to say how many people live on
each street. But let's simply count the colours of fruit :-)

```
my %data =
    apple => 'red',      avocado => 'green',
    banana => 'yellow', grapefruit => 'orange',
    grapes => 'green',   kiwi => 'green',
    lemon => 'yellow',   orange => 'orange',
    pear => 'green',     plum => 'purple',
;
```

By the way, notice that Raku is tolerant of the comma after the last value in
the hash initializer list.

Now it is time to count the statistics that we need.

```
my %stat;
%stat{$_}++ for %data.values;
say %stat;
```

The `values` method returns a list of all the values that the hash contains. In
the loop, they increment the values of the `%stat` hash. A new key is added
to `%stat` as soon as a new value from `%data` is seen. An increment of the
newly-created element sets the corresponding value to 1. Print the `%stat`
hash and see the result. Notice that the output data is not ordered.

```
{green => 4, orange => 2, purple => 1, red => 1, yellow => 2}
```

70. Product table

Generate and print the product table for the values from 1 to 10.

The task does not say anything about how to format the output.

First, let us print the results as a list with one line per one multiplication. In Raku, there is a cross operator X, which operates over lists and creates a cross product of them. Each element of the result list is a list of two elements coming from each of the operands of the X operator.

```
say "$_[0]×$_[1] = {[*] @$_}" for 1..10 X 1..10;
```

In each iteration, the loop variable $_ receives a list of two elements. They are printed inside the interpolated list: $_[0]×$_[1]. The string in double quotes also contains a block of code in curly braces, which is executed as a regular code.

The reduction operation is used here to multiply the two elements. Of course, it is possible to do multiplication directly: $_[0]*$_[1].

The output looks like this:

```
1×1 = 1
1×2 = 2
1×3 = 3
. . .
10×8 = 80
10×9 = 90
10×10 = 100
```

Now, let us print the result in the form of a table and try minimizing the code starting with two loops:

```
for 1..10 -> $x {
    for 1..10 -> $y {
        print $x * $y ~ "\t";
    }
    print "\n";
}
```

As the loop body of the inner cycle contains only one statement, it is possible
to rewrite it by using the postfix `for` loop:

```
for 1..10 -> $x {
    print "{$x * $_}\t" for 1..10;
    print "\n";
}
```

Finally, join the output using the `join` function, which also helps to eliminate
trailing tabulation characters at the end of lines:

```
for 1..10 -> $x {
    say join("\t", map {$x * $_}, 1..10);
}
```

It is also possible to call the functions as methods on lists:

```
for 1..10 -> $x {
    (1..10).map({$x * $_}).join("\t").say;
}
```

Further optimization isn't easy because two variables are needed for multiplication, while only one $_ can be used as a default loop variable. Now the
result is a proper table:

```
1  2  3  4   5  6  7  8  9  10
2  4  6  8   10 12 14 16 18 20
3  6  9  12  15 18 21 24 27 30
.  .  .
```

71. Pascal triangle

Generate the numbers of the Pascal triangle and print them.

The Pascal triangle is a sequence of rows of integers. It starts with a single 1 on the top row, and each following row has one number more, starting and ending with 1, while all of the other items are the sums of the two elements above it in the previous row. It is quite obvious from the illustration:

```
              1
             1 1
            1 2 1
           1 3 3 1
          1 4 6 4 1
        1 5 10 10 5 1
      1 6 15 20 25 6 1
```

To calculate the values of the next row, you may want to iterate over the values of the current row and make the sums with the numbers next to it. Let us use the functional style that the language offers.

Consider the fourth row, for example: **1 3 3 1**. To make the fifth row, you can shift all the values by one position to the right and add them up to the current row:

```
        1 3 3 1
  +     1 3 3 1
       1 4 6 4 1
```

In terms of arrays and assuming that the values of the fourth row are now contained in the @row variable, the calculations above are equivalent to the sum of the two arrays: current values in @row and a list of values that include 0 and all the values of @row. A trailing zero can be added to the current @row to make the arrays equally long.

This approach is illustrated by the following diagram:

```
    1 3 3 1 0
+   0 1 3 3 1
    1 4 6 4 1
```

Now, write that down in the Raku syntax using the technique from Task 53, *Adding up two arrays*.

```
@row = (|@row, 0) >>+<< (0, |@row);
```

Notice that the arrays are flattened with the help of a vertical bar: |@a. Without that, the (@row, 0) list is a list of two elements—an array and a scalar. Compare the output of the following test constructions:

```
my @row = 1, 2, 3;
say (@row, 0);   # ([1 2 3] 0)
say (|@row, 0); # (1 2 3 0)
```

Now, complete the program: we need to initialize the @row and add some printing instructions and create a loop:

```
my @row = 1;
say 1;
for 1..6 {
    @row = (|@row, 0) >>+<< (0, |@row);
    say @row.join(' ');
}
```

The program prints the first seven rows of the Pascal triangle. The rows are not centred and are aligned to the left side.

As an extra exercise, modify the program so that it prints the triangle as it is shown at the beginning of this task. For example, you can first generate rows and keep them in a separate array and then, knowing the length of the longest string, add some spaces in front of the rows before printing them.

Chapter 4

Regexes and Grammars

4.1

Regex matching

72. Count vowels in a word

Count the number of vowel letters in the given word.

Of course, we will abstract now from the difference between letters and sounds and will only count the number of vowel letters: a, e, i, o, and u.

```
my $word = 'Hello';
$word ~~ m:g:i/<[aeiou]>/;
say $/.elems;
```

Here, the given `$word` is matched against a regex that contains a character class with all the letters of our interest. Character classes in regexes use the `<[...]>` syntax. The regex is prefixed with the `:g` adverb, making it match as many times as needed to cover the whole string. The second adverb, `:i`, makes the regex case-insensitive.

The result of the match is a match object `$/`, which contains all the occurrences of vowel letters found in the word. Its length is the number we need. So, printing `$/.elems` gives the answer.

To extend the match to allow characters with diacritics, such as ü, the simplest is to add another adverb, `:m`, as shown in the next example.

```
$word = 'München';
$word ~~ m:g:i:m/<[aeiou]>/;
say $/.elems;
```

This program prints 2, as both ü and `i` matched.

If you prefer the long adverb names, here is the code:

```
$word ~~ m:global:ignorecase:ignoremark/<[aeiou]>/;
```

73. Count words

Count the number of words in a text.

Before solving the task, let us assume that by words we mean here a sequence of alphanumeric characters, including the underscore symbol.

Here is the solution:

```
my $text = prompt('Text> ');
say $text.comb(/\w+/).elems;
```

Try it on a few test inputs:

```
$ raku countwords.rk
Text> Hello, World;
2
```

The program uses regexes for extracting words using the \w character class and the `comb` string method that returns a sequence of the words:

```
$text.comb(/\w+/)
```

The + quantifier allows a repetition of \w, so it matches the whole word.

Alternatively, a more traditional match with a regex may be used:

```
$text ~~ m:g/(\w+)/;
say $/.elems;
```

Parentheses in the regex capture the word, and the `:g` adverb applies it a few times until all the words are found. The `$/` variable (called the *match object*) keeps all the matched substrings, and the `elems` method returns the number of elements in it.

74. Skipping Pod documentation

Create the program that copies the input text and skips the documentation in the Pod style that starts with =begin and ends with =end.

Let us take a simple text containing a piece of Pod documentation:

```
# Hello, World!
=begin
This program prints a message
=end
say 'Hello, World!';
```

The program should read it and print everything that is not the comment. Thus, for the given example, only the first and the last lines can go to the output.

There is a family of *flipflop* operators that, although being a bit hard to understand at first, are quite powerful for introducing the two-state triggers in the program flow.

```
while $_ = $*IN.get {
    .say unless /^'=begin'/ ff /^'=end'/;
}
```

Reading lines from the STDIN handle is the same as it will be done it in task 95, *The cat utility*. The flipflop construct /^'=begin'/ ff /^'=end'/ is False initially and becomes True as soon as the $_ content matches the first regex. After that, it stays True until the second condition is True.

In the end, the unless clause only passes the lines that are not located between the =begin and =end instructions. The .say method call is thus printing all the remaining lines.

75. Currency converter

Parse the string with a currency converting request such as '10 EUR in USD' and print the result.

The task of understanding free text is quite complicated. For the currency conversion, we can create a simple regex that matches the most common quires.

Let's ignore the way the exchange rate data are obtained and use the hard-coded values:

```
my %EUR =
    AUD => 1.4994,  CAD => 1.4741,
    CHF => 1.1504,  CNY => 7.7846,
    DKK => 7.4439,  GBP => 0.89148,
    ILS => 4.1274,  JPY => 131.94,
    RUB => 67.471,  USD => 1.1759;
```

This hash contains the exchange rates of a few currencies to Euro. Thus, it is possible to directly use it to get the results for any pair with EUR, such as:

```
10 EUR in GBP
20 ILS to EUR
```

For other combinations, a cross-rate can be used. For example, the request to convert JPY to CHF uses the values of JPY-to-EUR and EUR-to-CHF conversion.

Here is a regex that parses the textual request:

```
$request ~~
    /(<[\d .]>+) \s* (<:alpha> ** 3) .* (<:alpha> ** 3)/;
```

Let's also make a loop to accept multiple requests from the keyboard.

Here is the program:

```
while (my $request = prompt('> ')) {
    $request ~~
        /(<[\d .]>+) \s* (<:alpha> ** 3) .* (<:alpha> ** 3)/;
    my ($amount, $from, $to) = $0, $1, $2;

    my $result = 0;
    if $to eq 'EUR' {
        $result = $amount / %EUR{$from};
    }
    elsif $from eq 'EUR' {
        $result = $amount * %EUR{$to};
    }
    else {
        $result = $amount * %EUR{$to} / %EUR{$from};
    }

    say "$amount $from = $result $to";
}
```

After the regex match, the values are copied to the three variables: $amount, $from, and $to. The if—elsif—else chain is used to choose how the new amount is calculated: either as direct or cross rate.

Run the program and enter different requests with both integer and floating-point values for different combinations of the currency codes listed in the %EUR hash.

Here are a few ideas of how to improve the program:

1. Check if the entered currency code exists.
2. Make the request case-insensitive.
3. Create another hash with exchange rates against USD and choose it, whenever possible, to avoid cross-calculations.

Substitutions with regexes

76. Double each character

In a given string, double each alphanumeric character and print the result. Punctuation and spaces should stay untouched.

Regexes are very powerful tools for searching and replacing texts. In this task, only the alphanumeric characters are requested to be doubled. The \w character class is the perfect match to find these characters.

```
my $string = 'Hello, 1 World!';
$string ~~ s:g/(\w)/$0$0/;
say $string;
```

We are using the s/// construct here. The $string is matched against the \w regex. The parentheses around \w capture the found character. It is now contained in the $0 special variable.

In the second part of the replacement, $0 is used twice, and, thus, the doubled character is replacing the single character found in the string. The :g adverb makes the replacement global.

The program prints the following output:

```
HHeelllloo, 11 WWoorrlldd!
```

Let us update the program to exclude the r letter from the process. In other words, all the characters, except r, must be doubled. Build a new character class as a difference between \w and r as demonstrated in the following line of code:

```
$string ~~ s:g/(<[\w] - [r]>)/$0$0/;
```

Now, the output is a bit different: HHeelllloo, 11 WWoorldd!

77. Remove duplicated words

Remove repeated words from <u>from</u> a sentence.

Repeated words are most often unintended typing mistakes. In rare cases, though, this is correct like with the word *that*:

He said that that tree is bigger.

Anyway, let us remove the double words ignoring the grammar for now. To find if the word is repeated, a regex with variables can be used. Then, using a substitution, only one copy of a word is passed to the resulting string.

```
my $string = 'This is is a string';
$string ~~ s:g/ << (\w+) >> ' ' << $0 >> /$0/;


say $string;
```

The regex part of the s routine is a regex that is first looking for a word (as a sequence of word characters \w+) and its copy after a space. The first occurrence is saved in the $0 variable, which is immediately used in the same regex. It is also used in the replacement part.

To prevent repetitions, the word-edge anchors are used: << for the beginning of a word and >> for its end. In the given example, this prevents treating the last two letters of the word *This* as a separate word, *is*, and thus, the correct phrase *This is a string* will not be broken after the substitution.

Notice that non-literal spaces in a regex are not taking part in string matching, although, they are necessary in a sequence << (\w+) >>. The construction <<(\w+)>> is a syntax error as it is similar to the character class <[...]> or a reference to a named regex like <:alnum>, and the compiler prefers explicit spaces in this case.

78. Separate digits and letters

In a given string that contains letters and digits, insert dashes on the borders between the digit and letter sequences.

The goal of the task is to convert, for example, the string `6TGT68` to `6-TGT-68`. With some modification, this task may be needed for creating the canonical form of car license plates in some countries.

There are character classes in the Raku regexes: `<:alpha>` for alphabetical characters and `<:digit>` for digits. Let us use them for finding the borders between digits and letters. In other words, we need to find all the sequences of two characters, where one of them is a letter and another is a digit.

```
my $s = '6TGT68';

$s ~~ s:g/
    (<:alpha>) (<:digit>) |
    (<:digit>) (<:alpha>)
/$0-$1/;

say $s; # 6-TGT-68
```

The replacement construct `s:g///` is applied globally. It finds all the places, which match either `<:alpha> <:digit>` or `<:digit> <:alpha>`.

When the match is found, the `$0` and `$1` variables are set to either a letter and a digit or to a digit and a letter. The parentheses indices count from zero in each alternative separated with a vertical bar.

The replacement uses the found characters and inserts a hyphen character between them. Notice that the spaces in the regex are allowed and ignored, while the spaces in the replacement part are significant, so the `/$0-$1/` part should not contain additional spaces.

79. Separate groups of digits

Put commas between the three-digit groups in a big number.

The task is to print an integer number, for example, `1234567890`, in the form
of `1,234,567,890`.

Here is a possible solution that uses a lot of Raku facilities:

```
$n ~~ s/<?after \d> (\d ** 3)+ $/{$0.map(',' ~ *).join}/;
```

On the top level, we've got a substitution `s///`. The pattern is anchored to
the end of the string: `s/...$//`. From the end of the string, groups of three
digits are searched: `(\d ** 3)+`. A single `\d` matches a digit, and the `**`
quantifier requires exactly three of them. The second quantifier, `+`, allows
more than one such groups.

A dot may only follow at least one digit. To avoid converting six-digit numbers to something like `.123.456`, a look-behind assertion `<?after \d>` is
inserted, which insists that there is a digit before the first group of three
digits. The whole replacement only happens if there are more than four digits in the original number.

The second part of the substitution is an executable code: `s//{...}/`. After
a successful match, the three-digit groups appear in the match object `$0`.
Because of the + quantifier, you can treat this object as an array.

First, each element is translated to a string with a comma in front of it:
`map(',' ~ *)`. Using the * character creates a `WhateverCode` block, which
is equivalent to `{',' ~ $_}`. It is also possible to rewrite the map operation
using the string interpolation: `map({",$_"})`.

Finally, transformed parts are joined together, using the `join` method call.
The `$n` variable now contains a string with the desired result.

80. Increase digits by one

In the given integer number, replace all the digits so that 1 becomes 2, 2 becomes 3, etc., and 9 becomes 0.

This task can be approached both mathematically and string-wise. In Raku, regexes seem to be the best match. Although a number is an example of the numeric data type, the language allows seamless changes when you want to start working with them as with strings.

In the proposed solution, a number is matched against a regex.

```
my $number = 564378901;
$number ~~ s:g/ (\d) /{ ($0 + 1) % 10 }/;
say $number;
```

Similar to the code of Task 76, *Double each character*, a global replacement happens. The target is a digit, \d. (We ignore the fact that the \d character class matches 580 different characters in the Unicode space, see Task 39, *Unicode digits*.)

So, a digit (treated as a character) lands in the $0 variable. In the replacement part of s///, a block of code is placed. It takes the value of $0 and adds 1 to it. As the + operator expects numeric operands, the character is converted to an integer and is incremented after it. The modulo operator keeps the value in the range between 0 and 9 (including), The new value is converted back to a string character, which replaces the original digit that was captured.

In the given example, 675489012 is printed.

Notice that it was not possible to use an increment operator in the replacement. An attempt to make it $0++ would lead to an exception as the ++ operator needs a mutable object.

81. Pig Latin

Convert the given text to Pig Latin.

Pig Latin is a pseudo-language, each word of which is derived from the corresponding English word, following a couple of simple rules:

1. *If the word starts with consonant letters (including consonant sounds represented by letter combinations such as* qu*), move them all to the end of the word.*
2. *Append the* ay *ending.*

Here is a program that implements this algorithm.

```
my $text = prompt('English > ');


$text ~~ s:i:g/ << ([qu]? <-[aeiou]>+) (\w*) >> /$1$0/;
$text ~~ s:i:g/ << (\w+) >> /$0ay/;


say $text; # you are welcome → ouyay areay elcomeway
```

For simplicity, both steps are done via their own regex replacements. The first one finds the words that starts with either *qu* or with a character that is not a vowel (in other words, which is neither *a*, *e*, *i*, *o*, or *u*). The two captured parts of the word are switched in the replacement part: `$1$0`.

The second substitution instruction finds all the words (at this point, the words that had initially started with consonants are already modified and the words, starting with vowels, stay original) and appends the *ay* ending to it.

The `<<` and `>>` anchors bind the regexes to word borders.

As an exercise, modify the program to take care of capital letters in the original sentence so that *You* becomes *Ouyay* and not *ouYay*.

82. Simple string compressor

Convert a string containing repeating characters to a string, where each repetition is represented by the character and the number of its copies.

For example, the original string `abccccdefffffgggghhi` converts to the compressed string `abc4def5g3h2i`.

```
my $str = 'abccccdefffffgggghhi';

$str ~~ s:g/
        ( (<:alpha>) $0+ )
    /{
        $0[0] ~ $0.chars
    }/;

say $str; # abc4def5g3h2i
```

The global replacement finds the parts of the string with repeated characters. The tricky part in the regex is the way in which capturing parentheses are counted.

The naïve regex `<:alpha>+` matches any letter sequence and consumes the whole string. Thus, only one character must be captured: `(<:alpha>)`. Now, the regex should demand repetitions of that character: `$0+`, but we also need to capture it as we have to know the length of it.

It is not possible to say `(<:alpha>)($0+)`, as `$0` is referring to the capturing part in the second parentheses. The final regex contains nested capturing parentheses.

The `$0` match object keeps the whole repeated sequence and the array with one element that holds the first matched character. The replacement part uses both elements to build the result: `$0[0] ~ $0.chars`.

83. %Templating% engine

Implement a simple templating engine, which substitutes values in placeholders of the form %name%.

The objective is to create a function that takes a template string and a hash with named values and does the substitution. So, let us prepare and pass them to a function. Notice that, in Raku, it is possible to pass a hash as easy as you pass a scalar (see also Task 65, *Passing arrays to subroutines*).

```
my $template = 'Hello, %name%! Welcome to %city%!';
my %data = (
    name => 'Klara',
    city => 'Karlovy Vary',
);

say process_template($template, %data);
```

Inside the function, the hash is passed as a single hash variable.

```
sub process_template($template is copy, %data) {
    $template ~~ s:g/ '%' (\w+) '%' /%data{$0}/;
    return $template;
}
```

The function modifies the value of the first argument; this is why it is marked with the `is copy` trait.

The regex is global, which is turned on by the `:g` regex adverb. A regex is looking for words between the two percentage symbols. In Raku, non-alphanumeric characters must be quoted or escaped, so both `'%'` and `\%` are accepted. The second part of the replacement is using the matched value as the key for fetching the value from the `%data` hash.

4.3

Using grammars

84. Decode Roman numerals

Convert a string, with a Roman number, to a decimal number.

The task is opposite to Task 46, *Convert to Roman numerals*, but let's use grammars to solve it. The idea is to directly find the sequences of Roman digits that correspond to thousands, hundreds, tens, and ones. For example, as soon as the program sees LXX, it knows that it is equal to 70. We are not analysing which letters go on the left or right of the given one. Instead, the result is achieved directly.

Here is a complete program, the biggest part of which is the grammar class. It uses a global variable $n for accumulating the decimal number during the parsing.

```
my $n = 0;
grammar Roman {
    token TOP {
        <thousands>? <hundreds>? <tens>? <ones>?
    }

    token thousands {
        | M    { $n += 1000 }    | MM    { $n += 2000 }
        | MMM  { $n += 3000 }    | MMMM { $n += 4000 }
    }

    token hundreds {
        | C    { $n += 100 }     | CC    { $n += 200 }
        | CCC  { $n += 300 }     | CD    { $n += 400 }
        | D    { $n += 500 }     | DC    { $n += 600 }
        | DCC  { $n += 700 }     | DCCC { $n += 800 }
        | CM   { $n += 900 }
    }
```

```
    token tens {
            | X     { $n += 10 }      | XX    { $n += 20 }
            | XXX   { $n += 30 }      | XL    { $n += 40 }
            | L     { $n += 50 }      | LX    { $n += 60 }
            | LXX   { $n += 70 }      | LXXX  { $n += 80 }
            | XC    { $n += 90 }
    }

    token ones {
            | I     { $n += 1 }       | II    { $n += 2 }
            | III   { $n += 3 }       | IV    { $n += 4 }
            | V     { $n += 5 }       | VI    { $n += 6 }
            | VII   { $n += 7 }       | VIII  { $n += 8 }
            | IX    { $n += 9 }
    }
}

my $roman = 'MMXVIII';
Roman.parse($roman);
say $n;  # 2018
```

The TOP token of the grammar describes how the Roman number is built. A
Roman number is a sequence of thousands, hundreds, tens, and ones. All
these parts are optional: `<thousands>? <hundreds>? <tens>? <ones>?`.

Then, the grammar defines the tokens for each individual part. Their structure is similar: It is a set of alternatives; examine, for instance, the ones to-
ken: I | II | III | IV | V | VI | VII | VIII | IX.

Each branch of alternatives is equipped with a simple code block that updates the value of the global variable $n. To make the grammar reusable, add
the { $n = 0 } block at the beginning of TOP. As homework, convert the
grammar to use $/.make and $/.made methods of the match object to collect
the parts of the value without using a global variable.

85. Balanced parentheses

Check if the parentheses in a given string are balanced, i. e., whether every opening parenthesis has the corresponding closing one.

Let us limit the input strings with the strings containing parentheses () only and no other kinds of brackets {}, [], or <>. The text in between contains only letters and spaces. Empty parentheses are not allowed.

Prepare the test suite with different cases—a series of balanced examples and a series of strings with unbalanced parentheses.

```
my @tests = 'a',          '(a)',        '(a b c)', 'a (b)',
            '(b) a',       '(b (a))',    '( ( c))', 'a(b)c',

            'a (', 'a)', '(a) b c)', 'a b)',     '(b a',
            '((b (a))', '((c)',      '(((a(((', ')a(';
```

For such a task, the best tool available in Raku is grammars. Here is a simple grammar description that can recursively parse the above examples.

```
grammar Balanced {
    rule TOP {
        <expression>+
    }
    rule expression {
        | <:alpha>+ <expression>?
        | '(' ~ ')' <expression>
    }
}
```

The `TOP` rule says that the sentence is at least one `expression`. An `expression` is either a few letters (`<:alpha>+`) optionally followed by another `expression` or an `expression` in parentheses.

Notice the way parentheses are introduced in the `expression` rule:

```
'(' ~ ')' <expression>
```

This syntax allows keeping the opening and closing characters together and is synonymous with the following rule:

```
'(' <expression> ')'
```

Now we can parse the strings from the test suit with the `Balanced` grammar.

```
for @tests -> $test {
    my $result = Balanced.parse($test);
    printf("%-12s is%s balanced\n",
            $test,
            $result ?? '' !! ' not');
}
```

Depending on the success of parsing a string, the `$result` variable either contains a `Match` object or `Nil`. In the Boolean context, it is either `True` or `False`, and it defines what message is printed.

```
a            is balanced
(a)          is balanced
(a b c)      is balanced
a (b)        is balanced
(b) a        is balanced
(b (a))      is balanced
( ( c))      is balanced
a(b)c        is balanced
a)           is not balanced
(a) b c)     is not balanced
a b)         is not balanced
(b a         is not balanced
((b (a))     is not balanced
((c)         is not balanced
(((a(((      is not balanced
a (          is not balanced
)a(          is not balanced
```

86. Basic calculator

Create a program that calculates mathematical operations with two operands, for example: 4 + 5.3 or 7.8 / 3.

In this task, we will only limit the solution for the simplest case with only one operation so that there are no issues with the precedence order or parentheses.

Let's first make a solution with regexes and then transform it so it uses Raku's grammars.

```
my $expression = "14 * 16.4";
$expression ~~ /
    (<[-\d\.]>+) \s*
    ('+' | '-' | '*' | '/') \s*
    (<[-\d\.]>+)
/;
given $1 {
    when '+' {say $0 + $2}
    when '-' {say $0 - $2}
    when '*' {say $0 * $2}
    when '/' {say $0 / $2};
}
```

The regular expression in this example has three capturing parentheses. The first and the third of them match numbers with an optional minus sign and a floating-point dot. We do not check the number format too strictly to keep the program simple, however.

The construction <[...]> is a character class in Raku regexes. It lists accepted characters. In our case, those are the digits represented by \d, dots \., and minus -. Optional spaces around the operator are matched by \s*.

The operator character is an alternative: `'+' | '-' | '*' | '/'`.

After the successful match, the parts of `$expression` appear in the variables `$0`, `$1`, and `$2`. These are the shortcuts for the elements of the match objects: `$/[0]`, `$/[1]`, and `$/[2]`. Each element is also an object of the `Match` type.

The `given` statement chooses one of the `when` branches depending on the value in `$1`. Here, an implicit type conversion happens. First, the match object from `$1` is coerced to a string before comparing it with one of the operator characters. Second, the `$0` and `$1` objects are converted to numbers, which are used in actual calculations. Run the program a few times with different expressions and see how it works.

Now, let us solve the problem differently, using grammars. Here is the grammar:

```
grammar calc {
    rule TOP {
        <value> <operator> <value> {
            given $<operator> {
                when '+' {say $<value>[0] + $<value>[1]}
                when '-' {say $<value>[0] - $<value>[1]}
                when '*' {say $<value>[0] * $<value>[1]}
                when '/' {say $<value>[0] / $<value>[1]}
            }
        }
    }
    token value {
        '-'? \d+ [ '.' \d+ ]?
    }
    token operator {
        '+' | '-' | '*' | '/'
    }
}
```

And, here is how you use it to parse an expression:

```
my $expression = "14 * 16.2";
calc.parse($expression);  # Prints 226.8
```

The definition of the grammar contains the `TOP` rule and two tokens: `value` and `operator`. When the `parse` method is called, the grammar starts parsing the text, using the `TOP` rule, which says that the text should be a value, followed by the operator symbol, followed by another value.

This time, the regex for the values is a bit smarter to make sure the minus sign can appear only before digits, and the decimal point should be seen only once. Still, there is some room to improve the regex.

When using the grammar rules (such as `TOP`), you don't need to explicitly care about the optional spaces before parts of the expression. It means that both `'14 * 16.2'` and `'14*16.2'` strings are accepted.

The `TOP` rule has three parts: `<value> <operator> <value>`.

After they all match, the action code block is triggered. It contains a `given-when` block, similar to the one used earlier in the solution with regexes.

Now, the string values of the expression parts are taken from the match object, which is treated as a hash. For example, the operator character is located in the `$<operator>` object, which is a shortcut for `$/<operator>`. However, there are two `<value>`s in the `TOP` rule. In this case, the match object contains a list of other objects, which you can access via indices:

```
say $<value>[0] + $<value>[1]
```

Again, before using the values, the match objects are converted by Raku to numbers.

Part 2

Chapter 5

Date
and Time

87. Current date and time

Print current date and time as an epoch and in a human-readable format.

The `time` function returns the current time as the Unix epoch:

```
say time;
```

The output is something like this: `1495785518`.

For manipulating dates and times, use the built-in `DateTime` class:

```
say DateTime.now;
```

The date is now in a more human-readable format, although still is over-loaded with many details: `2017-05-26T10:02:20.500209+02:00`.

To access the separate elements of date and time, use the methods on the variable of the `DateTime` class:

```
my $dt = DateTime.now;

say $dt.day;     # 26
say $dt.month;   # 5
say $dt.year;    # 2017
say $dt.hour;    # 10
say $dt.minute;  # 9
say $dt.second;  # 5.55802702903748
```

The meaning of all the elements is quite straightforward.

All the values except seconds are integer. For the seconds, you may want to take the integer part only:

```
say $dt.second.Int;
```

88. Formatted date

Print the current date in an even better format.

There is a built-in `DateTime` class. It is equipped with a few useful methods, so there's no need to use external modules for many standard tasks. Save the current moment in the `$now` variable:

```
my $now = DateTime.now;
```

The easiest thing is to print the proper time using a dedicated method:

```
say $now.hh-mm-ss; # 22:37:16
```

To achieve a more granular control over both the date and time parts, use the `formatter` attribute of the constructor together with methods like `day` and `month` to get separate parts of the date and time (see Task 87, *Current date and time*):

```
my $now = DateTime.now(
    formatter => {
        sprintf '%02d.%02d.%04d, %02d:%02d',
        .day, .month, .year, .hour, .minute
    }
);

say $now; # 14.10.2017, 22:41
```

The formatting string `'%02d.%02d.%04d, %02d:%02d'` uses the standard POSIX `printf` format. The `sprintf` function forms a string that is returned when a `DateTime` object (the `$now` variable, in our case) is stringified. For instance, it is used when the variable is interpolated in a string:

```
say "Current date and time: $now.";
```

89. Datetime arithmetic

Find the difference between the two dates. Add a given number of days to the date.

The `DateTime` class defines the + and – operators, which can be used in combination with either another `DateTime` object or with the `Duration` object.

Let us first find the difference between the two given dates:

```
my $date1 = DateTime.new('2017-12-31T23:59:50');
my $date2 = DateTime.new('2018-01-01T00:00:10');

say $date2 - $date1; # 20
```

The type of the `$date2 - $date1` expression is `Duration`. In the numeric context, it returns the number of seconds. Therefore, there are 20 seconds between our dates at hand.

A `Duration` object can also be used instead of the second `DateTime` object.

For example, increase the given date by two minutes:

```
my $now = DateTime.now();
my $when = $now + Duration.new(120);
say "$now -> $when";
```

Or learn what were the date and time a week ago:

```
my $back = $now - Duration.new(3600 * 24 * 7);
say $back;
```

In the current design of the language, the constructor of the `Duration` class needs a number of seconds.

90. Leap years

Tell if the given year is leap or common.

The algorithm for detecting whether the year is leap includes a few divisibility tests. Take an extract in the pseudocode from Wikipedia:

if (year is not divisible by 4) then (it is a common year)
else if (year is not divisible by 100) then (it is a leap year)
else if (year is not divisible by 400) then (it is a common year)
else (it is a leap year)

It is possible to implement the above sequence of `if`s and `else`s in Raku, but it is a better idea to join conditions using the logical operators.

```
my $year = 2018;
say ($year %% 400 or $year % 100 and $year %% 4) ??
    'Leap' !! 'Common';
```

Notice that both the modulo `%` and divisibility `%%` operators are used, which allow avoiding Boolean negations in the sub-conditions.

The following program prints the list of leap years in the range 1800–2400:

```
for 1800 .. 2400 -> $year {
    say $year if $year %% 400 or $year % 100 and $year %% 4;
}
```

There may be some considerations regarding the efficiency of the sequence of the checks because each year is first tested against 400, while it may be more optimal to check first if the year is divisible by 4. If this becomes an important argument, then the `if-else` chain may be more efficient. To achieve an even higher speed, a pre-calculated array of leap years is better.

Chapter 6

Parallel Computing

91. Setting timeouts

Do not wait for a slow code block if it takes too long.

Promises are the best way to create timeouts. In the following example, two code blocks are created; they are executed in parallel.

```
my $timeout = Promise.in(2).then({
    say 'Timeout after 2 seconds';
});

my $code = start {
    sleep 5;

    say 'Done after 5 seconds';
}
```

Both `$timeout` and `$code` are the promises, i. e. objects of the `Promise` type. Actually, the `$timeout` variable is a promise that is executed as a result of keeping the anonymous promise created by the `Promise.in(2)` call. The `in` method of the `Promise` class creates a promise that becomes kept after the given number of seconds.

The second promise, stored in the `$code` variable, is created by the `start` function. This is a long-running code block, which does not return within five seconds. The `$code` promise can be kept only after that time.

The `$timeout` promise is kept earlier than the `$code` one. To let the program continue earlier, create another promise with the help of the `anyof` method:

```
await Promise.anyof($timeout, $code);

say 'All done';
```

The flow of the whole program is the following: first, the `$timeout` code block is created and starts running in a separate thread. Then, without waiting, the `$code` block has been created and launched. Finally, the next line of the main thread is executed; it creates an anonymous thread and waits until it is kept. The `await` routine blocks the execution of the main program until at least one of its arguments is kept. This program prints 'All done' after two seconds, and exits:

```
$ raku timeout.rk
Timeout after 2 seconds
All done
```

If the `$code` thread is completed first (say, if we changed the timeout value to 10 seconds), then the output is different, and the timeout is not triggered:

```
$ raku timeout.rk
Done after 5 seconds
All done
```

Keep in mind that in our examples, the program finishes after printing 'All done'. In case the program continues after that, the longest promise will still be running.

For example, add a simple delay like the one shown below:

```
await Promise.anyof($timeout, $code);
say 'All done';
sleep 20;
```

In this case, the program prints all three messages:

```
$ raku timeout.rk
Timeout after 2 seconds
All done
Done after 5 seconds
```

92. Sleep Sort

Implement the Sleep Sort algorithm for a few small positive integer values.

The *Sleep Sort* is a funny implementation of the sorting algorithm. For each input value, an asynchronous thread starts, which waits for the number of seconds equals to the input number and then prints it. So, if all the threads are spawned simultaneously, the output of the program contains the sorted list.

Here is the solution in Raku. On the next page, we will go through the bits of it and explain all the important moments.

```
await gather for @*ARGS -> $value {
    take start {
        sleep $value/10;
        say $value;
    }
}
```

Pass the values via the command line, and get them sorted.

```
$ raku sleep-sort.rk 9 10 2 8 5 7 6 4 1 3
1
2
3
. . .
8
9
10
```

The input values from the command line come to the @*ARGS array. The first step is to iterate over the array:

```
for @*ARGS -> $value {
    . . .
}
```

For each `$value`, the `start` block creates a promise with a code block that waits for the time that is proportional to the value and prints the value after that time.

```
start {
    sleep $value/10;
    say $value;
}
```

Dividing the value by ten speeds up the program. On the other hand, the delay should not be too small to avoid race conditions between different threads.

After a separate promise has been created for each input number, the program has to wait until all of them are kept. To achieve that, the `gather`—`take` construction is used. The `take` keyword adds another promise to a sequence, which is then returned as a whole by the `gather` keyword.

```
gather for @*ARGS -> $value {
    take start {
        . . .
    }
}
```

Finally, the `await` routine ensures the program does not quit until all the promises are kept or, in other words, until all the numbers are printed.

```
await gather . . . {
    take start {
        . . .
    }
}
```

93. Atomic operations

Using the solution for Task 38, the Monte Carlo method, *create a program that calculates the result using multiple threads.*

Raky comes with the built-in support for parallel computing. In Task 92, *Sleep Sort*, we've seen how to use the keywords `await`, `gather`, and `take` to spawn a few threads and wait for them to finish.

When different threads want to modify the same variable, such as a counter, it is wise to introduce atomic operations to make sure the threads do not interfere with each other. Here is the modification of the Monte Carlo program calculating the area of a circle with four parallel threads.

```
my atomicint $inside = 0;

my $n = 5000;
my $p = 4;

await gather for 1..$p {
    take start {
        for 1..$n {
            my @point = map {2.rand - 1}, 1..2;
            $inside⚛++ if sqrt([+] map *², @point) <= 1;
        }
    }
}

say 4 * $inside / $p / $n;
```

Run the program a few times, changing the value of $n (the number of random points per thread) and $p (the number of threads). The program should print the value that is close to π, such as `3.141524`.

The new thing here is the atomic increment operation:

```
$inside⚛++
```

An atomic operation ensures that the variable is modified with no conflicts
between the threads.

The variable itself should be a native integer of a special type—notice how
it is declared:

```
my atomicint $inside;
```

As the atomic operation uses the Unicode character, there is an ASCII alternative:

```
atomic-fetch-inc($inside)
```

Here's a list of other atomic operations and their synonyms that can be used
with parallel processes:

```
$var ⚛= $value          atomic-assign($var, $value)
my $a = ⚛$var           my $a = atomic-fetch($var)


$var⚛++                 atomic-fetch-inc($var)
$var⚛--                 atomic-fetch-dec($var)
++⚛$var                 atomic-inc-fetch($var)
--⚛$var                 atomic-dec-fetch($var)


$var ⚛+= $value         atomic-fetch-add($var, $value)
$var ⚛-= $value         atomic-fetch-dec($var, $value)
```

N. B. The code in this task works with the Rakudo compiler starting from
version 2017.09. Earlier versions do not support atomic operators.

94. Parallel file processing

Process the files from the current directory in a few parallel threads.

We have to do something with each file in the directory, and it has to be done in such a way that files are processed independently with a few workers. It is not possible to predict how long the process will take for each individual file, that's why we need a common queue, which supplies the filenames for the next available worker.

A good candidate for the queue is a channel.

```
my $channel = Channel.new();
$channel.send($_) for dir();
$channel.close;
```

All the file names are sent to the channel, which we close afterward. (On how to read directories, see more details in Task 97, *Reading directory contents*.)

Channels are designed to work thread-safe. It means that it is possible to get data from the channel using several threads, and each value is processed only once. Raku cannot predict which thread gets which name but it can guarantee that each data item is only read by the threads once.

```
my @workers;
for 1..4 {
    push @workers, start {
        while (my $file = $channel.poll) {
            do_something($file);
        }
    }
}
```

The code on the previous page creates four independent workers using the `start` keyword. As they are executed independently not only from each other but also from the main program, it is important to wait until all of them are done:

```
await(@workers);
```

The elements of the `@workers` array are promises (objects of the `Promise` data type). The `await` routine waits until all the promises are kept.

Another practical way of creating and waiting workers is shown in Task 92, *Sleep Sort*: instead of collecting them in an array, you can use the `gather` and `take` keywords.

Examine the main loop:

```
while (my $file = $channel.poll) {
    do_something($file);
}
```

On each iteration, a value from the channel is read. The `poll` method ensures that the reading stops after the channel is exhausted.

All four threads are doing similar work and are polling the same channel. This approach distributes the filenames that were sent to the channel between the workers. As a name has been read, it is removed from the channel, and the next read request returns the next name.

Finally, cook the `do_something` sub according to your needs. In the following simplest example, it only prints filenames:

```
sub do_something($file) {
    say $file.path;
}
```

Chapter 7

Miscellaneous

95. The `cat` utility

Create the equivalent of the UNIX cat utility that copies its STDIN input directly to STDOUT.

Reading from the input and sending it to the output is a relatively easy task. The `$*IN` handle is by default connected to STDIN. Being an object of the `IO::Handle` type, it has the `slurp` method that returns the whole input text in one go. What is left to do, is just to print it to the output, which defaults to STDOUT.

Here's the complete program:

```
say $*IN.slurp;
```

This works well, and we can use it via the command line:

```
$ raku cat.rk < file1.txt > file2.txt
```

However, in the interactive mode, the program does not replicate each entered line, but instead, it waits until the end of the output (say, until you press Ctrl+D). This behaviour is fully explainable because of the use of the `slurp` method.

Let us modify the program so that it prints each line as soon as it is entered. The `IO::Handle` class has another method, `get`, which reads one line from the handle and returns it. Create a loop and print the line after it is delivered by the `get` method:

```
.say while $_ = $*IN.get;
```

Here, the default variable `$_` is used. This allows to omit creating the new variable and to make the whole program more compact. The `.say` call in it is a shortcut for `$_.say`.

96. The `uniq` utility

Create the simple equivalent of the UNIX `uniq` utility, which only prints the lines from the STDIN input, which are not repeating the previous line.

The solution of this task can be built on the solution of Task 95, *The cat utility*. This time, the entered lines have to be saved, so let's introduce the `$previous` variable and make an explicit code block for the loop.

```
my $previous = '';
while (my $line = $*IN.get) {
    say $line unless $line eq $previous;
    $previous = $line;
}
```

On each iteration, the next line from the `$*IN` handle is read and saved in the `$line` variable. If the value is different from the previous line, which is saved in the `$previous` variable, then the current line has been printed.

At the moment, only duplicated lines are affected. If the two identical lines are separated by other lines, then everything is printed. Let us modify the program so that it only prints the unique lines per whole input stream.

```
my %seen;
while (my $line = $*IN.get) {
    next if %seen{$line};
    say $line;
    %seen{$line} = 1;
}
```

Here, the `%seen` hash is used as a storage of the lines printed. It's also a good practice to use a `Set` object instead; see the example of using a set in Task 54, *Exclusion of two arrays*.

97. Reading directory content

Print the file names from the current directory.

Reading a directory can be done using the `dir` routine defined in the `IO::Path` class.

```
say dir();
```

This tiny program does not do the task really satisfactory, as the `dir` routine returns a lazy sequence (an object of the `Seq` data type) of `IO::Path` objects.

To get the textual file names, take the path part of an `IO::Path` object using the `path` method:

```
.path.say for dir;
```

The code is equivalent to the more verbose fragment:

```
for dir() -> $file {
    say $file.path;
}
```

If you want to print full paths of the files in a directory, use the `absolute` method:

```
.absolute.say for dir;
```

The `test` named argument of the `dir` routine allows selecting filenames that match a certain regex, for example, listing all jpeg files:

```
for dir(test => /\.jpg$/) -> $file {
    say $file.path;
}
```

98. Text to Morse code

Convert the given text to the Morse code.

Converting text to the Morse code is a relatively easy task. The solution is to replace all the alphanumeric characters with the corresponding representation in the Morse code.

In this solution, all the other characters are ignored and are removed from the source string. In the Morse code, letters are separated by the duration of one dash, and words are separated by the duration of approximately 2.5 dashes, so in the program, one space is used for separating characters, and three spaces separate the words.

The above logic is programmed in the series of replacements. First, lower-case the whole phrase (there is no distinction between lower- and upper-case letters) and then remove all the non-alphanumeric characters and increase the distance between the words. Finally, replace each remaining printable symbol with the corresponding Morse sequence.

```
my %code = (
    a => '.-',       b => '-...',     c => '-.-.',
    d => '-..',      e => '.',        f => '..-.',
    g => '--.',      h => '....',     i => '..',
    j => '.---',     k => '-.-',      l => '.-..',
    m => '--',       n => '-.',       o => '---',
    p => '.--.',     q => '--.-',     r => '.-.',
    s => '...',      t => '-',        u => '..-',
    v => '...-',     w => '.--',      x => '-..-',
    y => '-.--',     z => '--..',     0 => '-----',
    1 => '.----',    2 => '..---',    3 => '...--',
    4 => '....-',    5 => '.....',    6 => '-....',
    7 => '--...',    8 => '---..',    9 => '----.'
);
```

```
my $phrase = prompt('Your phrase in plain text> ');

$phrase.=lc;
$phrase ~~ s:g/<-[a..z0..9]>/ /;
$phrase ~~ s:g/\s+/   /;
$phrase ~~ s:g/(<[a..z0..9]>)/%code{$0} /;

say $phrase;
```

Let us test this on a random phrase:

```
$ raku morse.rk
Your phrase in plain text> Hello, World!
.... . .-.. .-.. ---   .-- --- .-. .-.. -..
```

The conversion table takes the biggest part of the program.

The regexes show how character classes are created.

A characters class with a range of symbols:

```
<[a..z0..9]>
```

A negative character class, which matches with any character other than the
one from the range:

```
<-[a..z0..9]>
```

These character classes list all the allowed characters that can be encoded
by the given %code hash. It is also possible to use \w and \W or <alnum> and
<!alnum> instead of the above regexes if you are sure that the input string is
pure ASCII.

All the regexes in the program come with the :g adverb to make them global.
Regex matching uses the double tilde ~~ operator for both matching and
replacement.

99. Morse to text

Convert the Morse sequence to plain text.

To save efforts in typing the decoding table, we can use the `%code` hash from Task 98, *Text to Morse code*, and create the 'inversed' hash, where the keys are the Morse sequences, and the values are letters or digits:

```
my %char = %code.kv.reverse;
```

Printing this variable shows its contents in the following way:

```
{- => t, -- => m, --- => o, ----- => 0, ----. => 9, ---.. => 8,
--. => g, --.- => q, --.. => z, --... => 7, -. => n, -.- => k,
-.-- => y, -.-. => c, -.. => d, -..- => x, -... => b, -.... => 6,
. => e, .- => a, .-- => w, .--- => j, .---- => 1, .--. => p,
.-. => r, .-.. => l, .. => i, ..- => u, ..--- => 2, ..-. => f,
... => s, ...- => v, ...-- => 3, .... => h, ....- => 4, ..... => 5}
```

Despite the fact that the output does not include the quotes, all the keys and values in `%char` are strings. The next step is to replace the sequences from the keys of the hash with its values. The small difficulty is that, unlike the text-to-Morse conversion, a regex has to search for the sequence of a few characters (dots and dashes), so it must anchor to the boundaries of the Morse characters.

The built-in `<<` and `>>` regex anchors for word boundaries assume that the words are sequences of letters and digits, while Morse sequences are dots and dashes. Let's use a space to serve as a separating character. To simplify the task, just add an additional space to the string before decoding it.

```
my $text = prompt('Morse phrase> ') ~ ' ';
$text ~~ s:g/(<[.-]>+) ' '/%char{$0}/;
$text ~~ s:g/\s+/ /;
say $text;
```

100. Brainfuck interpreter

Create the interpreter for the Brainfuck language.

Brainfuck is an esoteric programming language that has a small set of instructions, each of them a single punctuation character.

It is assumed that the Brainfuck program has built-in data memory, which is an array of integers, and a pointer to the currently selected item. The two instructions, + and -, increment and decrement the current element. The < and > instructions move the data pointer one position to the left or to the right.

Another two instructions, . and ,, either print the current element using its values as the ASCII codepoint (in theory, it can be Unicode) or read a character from the standard input and put its numeric value to the current element of the data array.

Finally, [and] create loops. If when the program reads the closing bracket character, the current data element is not zero, the program returns to the corresponding opening bracket. In the case the program reads an opening bracket and the current data element is zero, the whole block between the two matching brackets is skipped. This option can also be used for embedding comments.

All other characters are ignored. This gives the ability to separate the program instructions with spaces or newlines, as well as to add comments just next to the main code. The comments should simply not include the main characters used as the code instructions.

Online, you can find many examples of the Brainfuck code. We'll test our program on the following 'Hello World!' program:

```
+++++++++[>+++++[>++>+++>+++>+<<<<-]>+>+>->>+[<]<-]>>.>---
.+++++++..+++.>>.<-.<.+++.------.--------.>>+.>++.
```

Now, we are ready to create the interpreter of Brainfuck in Raku.

First, read the source code to the $program variable, and pass it to the main interpreter subroutine:

```
my $program = $*IN.slurp;
brainfuck($program);
```

The parser first creates the containers it needs for the process: @program holds the program as an array of characters; the $program_pointer is set to the beginning of it; @data_memory keeps the data, and its current position is also set to 0 via $data_pointer.

```
sub brainfuck($program) {
    my @program = $program.comb('');
    my $program_pointer = 0;
    my @data_memory;
    my $data_pointer = 0;
```

Now, iterate over the program instructions.

```
    while $program_pointer < @program.elems {
```

At this point of the main loop, the @program[$program_pointer] element contains the current program instruction. We are using the given—when block to understand the meaning of it and make an action. The first four commands are straightforward:

```
        given @program[$program_pointer] {
            when '>' {$data_pointer++}
            when '<' {$data_pointer--}
            when '+' {@data_memory[$data_pointer]++}
            when '-' {@data_memory[$data_pointer]--}
```

Let's skip the comma command for now and move on to the input dot. The input command is using the @data_memory array and the chr method to translate codepoints to characters.

```
when '.' {
    print @data_memory[$data_pointer].chr
}
```

Finally, the loop commands [and]. Their behaviour depends on the value of the current data element @data_memory[$data_pointer]. If the condition is met (i. e., if the current element is zero for [and non-zero for]), the $program_pointer must be moved to the position of the matching bracket.

To simplify the program, the code to find balancing brackets is placed to separate functions, _move_forward, and _move_back. They modify the value of the program pointer, which is passed as an argument.

```
when '[' {
    $program_pointer =
        _move_forward(@program, $program_pointer)
    unless @data_memory[$data_pointer];
}
when ']' {
    $program_pointer =
        _move_back(@program, $program_pointer)
    if @data_memory[$data_pointer];
}
}
```

All other instructions, which are not listed in the when clauses, are simply ignored. After the current instruction has been processed, the program pointer is moved to the next position:

```
$program_pointer++;
    }
}
```

Finally, here is the code for the functions searching balancing brackets. They move either forward or backwards and count the opening and closing brackets. The `$level` variable is increased if the program finds the bracket, which is not the correct pair.

```
sub _move_back(@program, $program_pointer is copy) {
    my $level = 1;
    while $level && $program_pointer >= 0 {
        $program_pointer--;
        given @program[$program_pointer] {
            when '[' {$level--}
            when ']' {$level++}
        }
    }
    return $program_pointer - 1;
}


sub _move_forward(@program, $program_pointer is copy) {
    my $level = 1;
    while $level && $program_pointer < @program.elems {
        $program_pointer++;
        given @program[$program_pointer] {
            when '[' {$level++}
            when ']' {$level--}
        }
    }
    return $program_pointer - 1;
}
```

The subroutines use the same approach with the given—when keywords for dealing with command characters as in the main loop.

To prevent infinite loops in case of the incorrect program, both subs check if the `$program_pointer` reaches the beginning or end of the program. Notice that because the `$program_pointer` is modified inside the subs, it is declared as `is copy` in the signatures of the subs. The return value is intentionally decremented by one to compensate the subsequent increment of it in the main loop: `$program_pointer++`.

The interpreter is complete. Save the 'Hello World!' program in a file and pass it in the command line:

```
$ raku brainfuck.rk < helloworld.bf
Hello World!
```

As an exercise, modify the interpreter so that it understands the , command. You need to update the **given**—**when** list in the main loop with the code that reads the character from the input:

```
when ',' {@data_memory[$data_pointer] = $*IN.getc.?ord}
```

The `$*IN.getc` returns `Nil` when there are no more characters in the input. Try to catch this situation to avoid filling the data memory with empty data. Here is a test program that copies the input to the output:

```
>+[[>],.-------------[+++++ +++++ +++[<]]>]<<[<]>>[.>]
```

Another useful modification would be error handling. There are a few places in the program where increments or decrements in one of the pointers may go out of the array ranges. Add the code that checks that to display an error message. To make the process easier, use some simple debugging code like the one below to visualise the position of the program pointer and data state at each iteration of the main loop:

```
say $program;
say ' ' x $program_pointer ~ '^';
say @data_memory[0..$data_pointer - 1] ~ ' [' ~
    @data_memory[$data_pointer] ~ '] ' ~
    @data_memory[$data_pointer + 1..*];
```

What's next?

Congratulations on finishing the book!

The 100 tasks that you were working with are among the first challenges that you encounter when learning a programming language. Although some of the solutions required many lines of code—that was only the beginning.

Keep experimenting and make your way in running the Raku code in production applications!

Andrew Shitov
Amsterdam, 13 October 2019

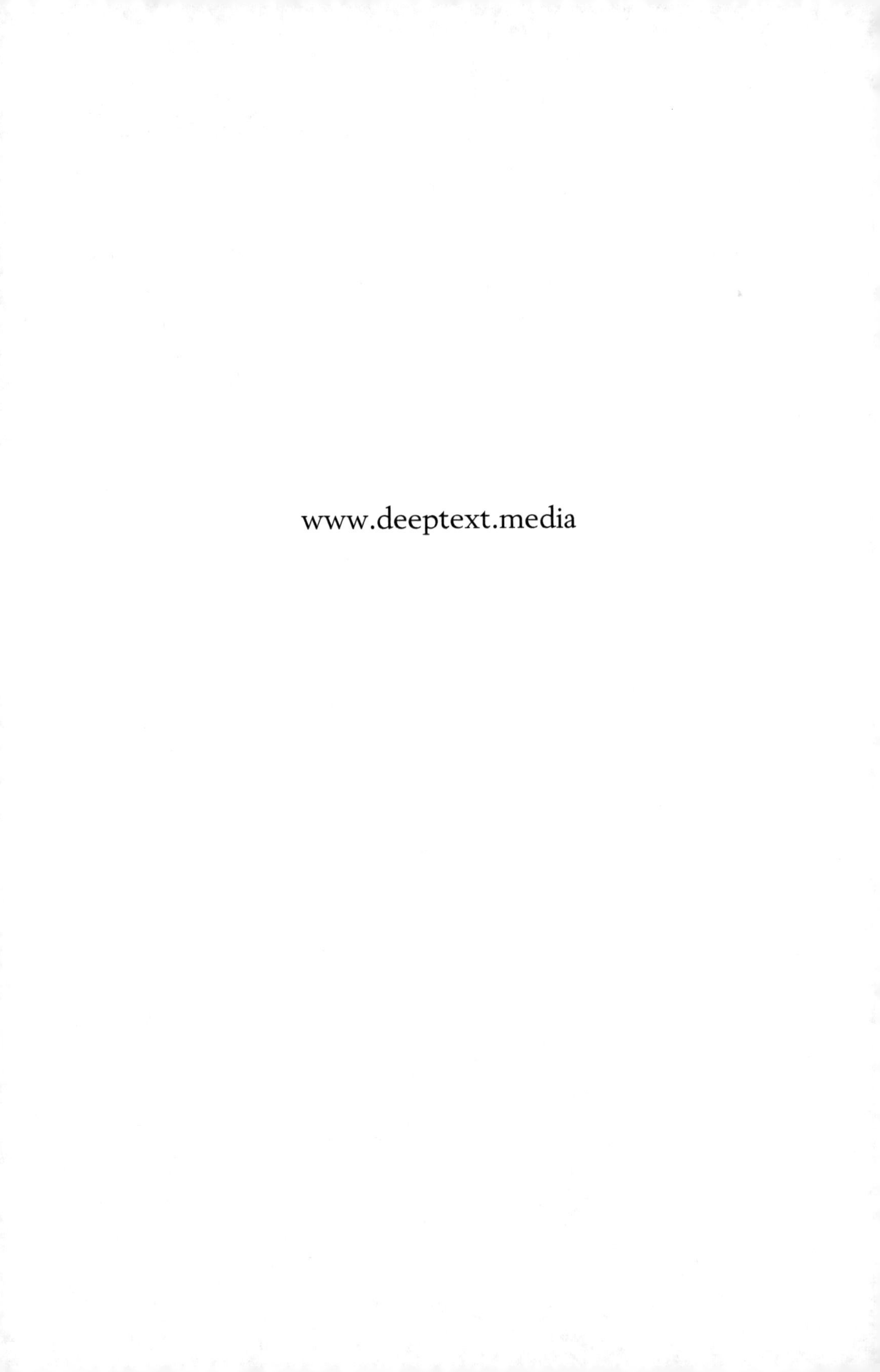